"Miss de Havilland Tells All . . ."

—Chicago Tribune

About:

"Her seven-year stint as Mme. Pierre Galante, a sharp-eyed Franco-U.S. housewife and what she found out about French husbands . . . a happy Jean Kerr–ish account . . . a funny one . . ."

—Life

About:

"An unending battle with law, custom, society, fashion . . . sales clerk and landlord . . . Who laughs last laughs best. She does and you along with her."

—New York Herald Tribune

Results:

"A rib-tickler . . . excellent."

—New York Mirror

"Lively and pleasant . . . wicked and roguish."

—Oakland Tribune

"Nostalgic, provocative."

—New York Times

Every

Frenchman

Has

One

By Olivia de Havilland

CROWN
ARCHETYPE
NEW YORK

All rights reserved.
Published in the United States by Crown Archetype,
an imprint of the Crown Publishing Group, a division of
Penguin Random House LLC, New York.
crownpublishing.com

Crown Archetype and colophon is a registered trademark of
Penguin Random House LLC.

Originally published in slightly different form in the
United States by Random House, Inc., an imprint of
Penguin Random House LLC, in 1961.

Portions of this book have appeared in *McCall's Magazine*.

Library of Congress Cataloging-in-Publication Number: 62-12725

ISBN 978-0-451-49739-0
eBook ISBN 978-0-451-49740-6

Printed in the United States of America

Jacket design by Muriel Nasser
Jacket photograph © John Engstead/mptvimages.com
Case design by Elena Giavaldi

10 9 8 7 6 5 4 3 2 1

First Crown Archetype Edition

TO R. *Because you said*
"You should."

TO F. *Because you said*
"You must."

TO J. *Because you said*
"Why don't you?"

TO P. *Because you said*
"Voilà la machine à écrire.
Faites-le!"

Contents

About the Author

Olivia de Havilland began her film career at the age of eighteen playing Hermia in Max Reinhardt's motion picture presentation of Shakespeare's *A Midsummer Night's Dream*. Her films include *The Adventures of Robin Hood*, *Gone with the Wind*, *The Snake Pit*, and *Hush . . . Hush, Sweet Charlotte*. Over the course of her esteemed career, she has won two Academy Awards (for her leading roles in *To Each His Own* and *The Heiress*), as well as two New York Critics Awards, two Golden Globes, and a National Board of Review Award. In 2008, she received the National Medal of Arts, and in 2010, the French Legion of Honour. She lives in Paris.

*I'm not at all sure if you
know that I'm alive . . .*

I

I never will forget the day I went to see a movie which
you know all about if you've been watching television
lately: *Anthony Adverse.* I won't mention the year I saw
it, but it had just come out, and I was in it, and I was just
nineteen. I went in the afternoon, to the very first mati-
nee at Grauman's Chinese Theatre in Hollywood. Because I'd been in films only a year and this was the fifth
and best I'd so far made, I was very thrilled and excited,
sitting in the dark waiting for the picture to begin. I
was also enjoying the rest, because, as you've surmised,
I was just a little overworked.

The grand moment came, and with treble voice, her
hair hanging down her back, Angela, the character I
played, made her first appearance. As she did so, I heard
a lady behind me exclaim to another beside her, "That's
Olivia de Havilland!"

There followed a silence disturbed only by the muted

flapping of my ears. Then the second woman queried, "I wonder how old she is?"

There was no silence this time as the first lady replied with promptness and with certitude, "Why, she's thirty if she's a day!"

This incident has marked me, and because of it I'm not at all sure if you know that I'm alive. I have the idea that anyone who has ever heard my name has the distinct impression that I was put under the sod years ago just before they buried Lillian Russell. And so, when I wonder if you know that I live in France, I'm sure you don't, because I am certain that you think me peacefully interred, and in good old native American soil.

If that's the case, you're in for a surprise. By golly, I'm alive, all right, and I do live in France, and not under but on top of solid Parisian limestone. Furthermore, I speak First Class Foreign French, and if I've stunned you into immobility by all this startling information, you just keep seated and keep quiet, and I'll tell you how it all came about.

About nine years ago I was living (yes, even then) a life both sober and sobered, although conducted in Hollywood. I had very regretfully come to realize that a divorce from my first husband was necessary, and in August of 1952 had filed for and been granted an interlocutory decree of divorce. In the early spring of 1953 a film I'd been in, *My Cousin Rachel*, had just come out, and I was staying very much at home reading scripts for another one and keeping my eye on the apple of my eye, my three-year-old son, Benjamin Briggs Goodrich. If that sounds like a feat, it was, as he is the most active apple I have ever encountered.

While I was thus engaged, Louella was unhappy, Hedda was unhappy, and the publicity department at

Fox, where I'd made *Rachel*, was unhappy. They wanted me to fall in love. And you don't do that if you stay at home with your nose in a script and your eye on its apple, because, among other things, you are just too contorted to do so. Louella, Hedda, my agent, and Fox just didn't understand; they wagged their heads and remarked sadly, "There's only one male she loves, and that's Ben."

About six thousand miles away, on the other side of the Atlantic, the French government was busying itself with its usual occupations and, in addition, preparing for the Cannes Film Festival. As the chestnut trees along the Champs Élysées were getting ready to bloom, the office of the Secrétaire Général put a lot of white envelopes in the mail; one of them was addressed to me.

When it arrived at my Hollywood apartment, I deflected my gaze from Benjamin for a moment and read the enclosed invitation. I'd never been to France and I'd never been to a Festival, and after a fifth of a second of solemn deliberation I decided to accept. Forthwith I sent a message to the French government, which had graciously agreed to provide my transportation to and from the Festival, that I'd be happy to come if it would send me two airplane tickets instead of one.

Do you know, that simple, frank little request absolutely rocked the French government? And it's a government that's had its ups and downs. The Secrétaire Général of the Festival went right over to see the Secrétaire Général of *Paris Match*, France's most celebrated illustrated magazine, because the Secrétaire Général of *Paris Match* had actually been to Hollywood and had actually met some American actresses on home ground and could, no doubt, give some advice about my request. He could and he did. Seeing straight through my petition and seeing no reason why the French government should subsidize American romance, he said with clear, cogent brevity, *"Non."*

So while Louella and Hedda were shocked because I was not in love, two French Secrétaire Générals were shocked because I was. When I wasn't.

When the Secrétaire Général of the Festival finally learned that my proposed companion, though male, was exactly three and a half years old, his French family spirit came to an immediate and joyful boil, and without further ado and by fastest courier he dispatched to me two airplane tickets instead of one.

A month later, as the plane bringing Ben and me to France circled over Orly Field in the midmorning mid-April sunshine, I speculated as to what the very first Frenchman I would meet would be like. Unquestionably, he'd be dapper, with an Adolphe Menjou mustache. Naturally, he'd be gay, effervescent; he'd gesticulate. He'd be voluble in French, expressive in English. Of course he would kiss my hand. And that would be charming.

The plane landed and Ben and I emerged into the tonic, sun-filled air. We descended the ramp while the 580,000 photographers who hospitably greet each arriving Festival guest flashed every one of their 2,000,000 flash bulbs. Then we approached the air terminal door where my American, German-born, French-speaking agent was waiting for us. He was in Europe on business, and because I didn't know a word of French, he had come to see me through my first hours on foreign soil. With him was a Frenchman. The very first Frenchman I met in France. Handsome but hangdog. Cleanshaven and solemn. Didn't speak English, didn't even speak

French. And did not kiss my hand. He was the Secrétaire Général of *Paris Match*.

We met again forty-eight hours later at Cannes, in the revolving door of the Carlton Hotel. I was on my way to the opening night of the Festival and so was he. I wore a pink evening gown, long gloves and mink; he wore dinner clothes and his hangdog expression. More intense, though. Sort of hangdog *and* sheepish. He did not speak English, he did not speak French, and he did not kiss my hand.

My seat at the Palais du Festival throughout the festivities was always reserved, always the same—in the dress circle, one in from the aisle. Who was on the aisle? Every night, every performance, in his own reserved seat? The Secrétaire Général of *Paris Match*.

At the great supper parties after every film, at no matter whose table I sat, oddly enough, always beside me in his unreserved seat was the same singular Frenchman. Then at the Austrian Gala his expression changed. He smiled. Then he spoke. Fluently. In French, which I did not understand. Then in English, which I did. But he still did not kiss my hand—he held it in the taxi going home.

This opening skirmish swiftly developed into a major campaign, international in scale, range, and implication. As soon as the Festival was over I withdrew with my three-year-old aide-de-camp to England. We were overtaken. We retreated behind and beyond the national boundaries of the United States, even unto the heart of Texas.

Retrenched in Dallas, I went into rehearsal for *The Dazzling Hour*, a play which, by the way, was not to be presented in Dallas at all but in La Jolla, California.

That's hard to follow, I know, but it involves José Ferrer, the very mention of whose name will make clear any confusion. You know Joe—if there's anything he hates to do it's one thing at a time; in Dallas he was acting, singing, dancing and joking in *Kiss Me, Kate*, rehearsing *The Dazzling Hour*, and getting married. And in Dallas, even though the eyes of Texas were upon him, the one-man French Expeditionary Force made an airborne landing.

I fled, aide-de-camp and all, to La Jolla. Again we were routed. In Los Angeles my aide nearly reversed the field when, by the merest hazard, in the high spirits of healthy American youth, he struck the opposition an accidental blow on the top of the head with a potato masher. However, as August 26 came around my divorce became final, the adversary pursued his advantage undaunted, and by the end of the month, as one of the most intense and relentlessly fought operations in French military history came to a close, the tricolor rose triumphantly in the California sunshine over the Shoreham Apartments and I announced my engagement to Pierre Galante.

A few weeks later the victor set sail for his native shore in the barque the *Liberté*, and at the same time, by merest coincidence, Air France sent me an invitation to christen and be aboard their inaugural Chicago–Paris nonstop flight. Needless to say, enclosed with the invitation were two airplane tickets instead of one.

I planted my own standard on the Left Bank of the River Seine in late October of 1953, and though I have since transferred it to the Right Bank, it has been fluttering with considerable joy and gaiety from that first moment to this one. My aide-de-camp is now twelve years old, and because settling down in a foreign country requires quite a bit of staff work, Pierre and I have given him an assistant. She is now five years old, is named Gisèle, and has all the requisites for a happy life that any girl could ask for: a full set of teeth, pretty legs, and a mouth like a kiss. She thinks her brother is God, and he is leaving it that way.

We live in Paris in a little white house which is as tall and narrow as a chimney; behind it we have a little garden with our own chestnut tree and a small fountain for the pigeons and sparrows to bathe in. Just as you've supposed, we are living happily ever after. In other words, to put it in a manner much more à la mode, I have made, toward living in a foreign country, a "very good adjustment." However, I've had my adventures, I can tell you, and if you'll just turn the page, you'll learn all about them.

I was definitely
under surveillance

2

When I set about to marry Pierre, I encountered French law for the first time, and, behind it, a kind of exactness and foresight which makes American law seem positively naïve and unimaginative.

When I met Pierre for the first time, in April, 1953, I was, as you know, a three-quarter divorcée. And when he followed me back to the States that summer, I became, as August passed, and as you also know, a full-fledged divorcée, with all the accruing rights, freedoms and privileges. So thought the state of California. So thought the Federal government of the United States of America. So thought I.

Two months later, in Paris, as I laid plans to make June out of January, I discovered that the United States might let me, a one-hundred-proof divorcée, remarry, but the French government wasn't about to. I found I was not under parole, exactly, but I was definitely under surveillance. For the best part of the year following the final decree of divorce, I was expressly forbidden by French law to remarry. I asked why. "Just in case," was the reply, "of an overly sentimental farewell with the previous husband on the day of the final decree." The period of surveillance is exactly nine months.

So when I returned to the United States to make *Not as a Stranger* for Stanley Kramer and United Artists in Hollywood, I explained to my curious friends why they would still have to wait awhile before they could call me Madame.

Charles Brackett, who had produced *To Each His Own*, in which I'd won my first Oscar, was vastly amused by my predicament, as he'd lived in France for some time before becoming one of Hollywood's best producer-writers, and already knew something of French custom and law.

"In France, in the case of twins, which of the twins is regarded as the senior, having primary rights of heredity?" he asked me.

"The first to be born," I replied with my American pragmatism.

"Not at all," corrected Charlie. "It's the second born. On the theory that the last to get out was the first to get in."

My husband's full name is Pierre Paul Galante. If we should ever have twin boys, and name them after their father, and I have them in France, we shall certainly be robbing Peter to pay Paul.

This sort of precise, but to us Americans somewhat inverse, logic of French law, is true of all sorts of aspects of French life, as I found out when *Not as a Stranger* was finished and I flew back to France to rejoin Pierre—this time, by the way, with my period of surveillance well (and satisfactorily) over, and perfectly free to marry under French law.

My plane arrived at Orly Field in the late afternoon of December 24, and as I descended the ramp, I found not only Pierre there to greet me, but a foreign representative of United Artists as well—the saddest-looking Frenchman I have ever seen.

"Oh, Miss de Havilland," he said sorrowfully, "what a sad time for you to be coming back to France." I hadn't read the papers for days, so I had no idea what national disaster might have taken place during my absence. Blanching, I asked why. "Because," he replied, "the French Customs is on strike." At this, thinking of my seven suitcases, I brightened and remarked that I was sorry that the strikers were having problems on Christmas Eve, but I failed to see how a strike among the Customs inspectors could be regarded as a disadvantage to the arriving traveler. "You don't understand," said the Frenchman, now quite ashen. "In France, when the Customs go on strike, it doesn't mean that they *refuse* to examine your luggage, it means that they examine *everything*!"

And then, because it was Christmas Eve, the strikers decided to do it the American way after all!

A few weeks later, with our wedding preparations proceeding in high gear, Pierre and I went to a dinner party with some charming and nimble-witted French friends, among whom were a brilliant lawyer and a cabinet minister.

After dinner the lawyer and the minister drew me aside and said they felt it was their duty to inform me of the rights I would enjoy, married to a Frenchman and living in France. "Now," said they, "if Pierre should be unfaithful, and if, in spite of your Anglo-Saxon heritage, a flash of Latin passion should overcome you, and you should shoot him, you will have nothing to worry about—you are perfectly certain to be let off absolutely free. But," they continued, noting my reassured expression, "if you marry a *second* Frenchman, and if *he* should be unfaithful, and if you should shoot *him*, then in that case it won't be *quite* so easy!"

Every Frenchman
has one

3

One thing not a single American traveler mentioned to me before I set out for France the first time, was the French liver. No book, no travel folder, had ever referred to this most significant of all human organs as far as the French constitution is concerned. Constitution with a small *c*, of course, although it is probably referred to in the one which begins with a big *C*, too. It's of that sort of importance.

Living in California, I knew, of course, that some Americans did have a liver. But they were usually hard drinkers and developed cirrhosis of the liver. I had the distinct impression that you developed first the liver, then the cirrhosis. Otherwise, you just had a stomach, which sometimes gave you stomach trouble, or stomach upset, or ulcer of the stomach. You might also have a bilious attack, which originated in and affected the stomach, of course. Now I know better. When Pierre finally got me definitely established on French soil, he set about filling in the appalling gaps in my education. He instructed me regarding the liver.

Every Frenchman has one. Every serious Frenchman takes good care of his own and gives advice regarding his neighbor's. A really patriotic Frenchman takes a cure every year, and if possible goes to a foreign spa to do so, showing himself to his European cousins as a responsible Frenchman.

My husband told me that a stomach upset was really *mal au foie*. He told me that if one had a runny nose and a slight cough, it was a sign of *un foie congestionné*. He also told me that if you threw up after eating too much cream, the chances were that you were suffering from an *intoxication du foie*. Eggs were bad for the *foie*. Milk was dreadful for the *foie*. Chocolate was pure poison. One evening at a dinner party, a Frenchwoman told me she had *un rhume de foie*. My husband hadn't spoken to me about that. I asked her not to mention it to him and please not to go near him either. When I thought of his poor *foie*, and all it had gone through—the congestion, intoxication, and the *mal* it had suffered—I just couldn't bear the idea of its catching cold, too.

Well, after we were married, my husband, who falls into the responsible class of Frenchmen, took me off to a foreign country for a cure. We went to Montecatini, northern Italy, near Florence. We established ourselves in a magnificent hotel called La Pace, unpacked our bags, and awaited the doctor. He came, asked us various questions about our health, probed our livers, put his perfumed head on our bosoms to listen, so I thought, to the heart and lungs, but now I realize he must have been listening to the liver too. Anyway, he commented that he had found my husband's liver to be just a little large, just a little hard. Pierre went white, but he pulled himself together and with a steady hand took from the doctor a sheaf of instructions made out specifically for his case. I took mine.

The next morning we rose early, dressed hastily, and walked up the avenue to a huge pink marble pavilion. Here we each bought a glass cup with quantities marked in grams on the side, and to the music of a sixteen-piece orchestra playing away among the Corinthian columns, we read our instructions and went to the appropriate marble counter for the appropriate water.

Montecatini, you see, is situated on volcanic springs of warm mineral water. Several types of mineral water—of varying properties and effects and strength. The water is piped directly to the vending temples (what else can you call them?), where they spurt out of a series of soda fountain dispensers operated by young girls dressed in blue-and-white striped dresses. According to your personal prescription you take one or two glasses of Tettuccio, Torretta, Rinfresco, or Tamerici, hot, cold, or indifferent, and you drink it in two minutes or five. The whole thing about which, how much, how long, and how hot is an exact science, so they say.

Well, my husband and I drank our Tettuccio, hot or cold as the case was, waited fifteen minutes as prescribed before we filled our glasses again with Rinfresco or Tamerici, drank that as we were supposed to, waited another fifteen minutes before the final glass of Torretta. Then we dashed. Back to the hotel. In the nick of time. Ten minutes later we were in the vine-hung courtyard of the hotel having Swiss rolls, honey and coffee, and our cure was completed for the day. The drinking and dashing part, that is.

At about ten we went to the baths. I don't quite understand why you take a radioactive bath when all the world is terrified of going out into the rain these days because there's too much strontium 90 in it for safety. But anyway you take a radioactive bath. It's green. They start you slowly with two bottles of radioactive water mixed into the tap water and you work up during the series to six. After each bath you rest for forty-five minutes, swathed in a warm sheet and lying on a couch. A radioactive bath is supposed to be very tiring. As I say, I don't quite know why you take it. Now, the next day you repeat the water-drinking program, but you take a different bath—carbonated this time. That is to say, a bath in what appears to be 7 Up. This is not so tiring, so you rest only five minutes afterward.

Back at your hotel after the 7 Up bath, you have a massage. It's the best of your life.

Then you have a cup of tea and descend to the great dining hall with its immaculate waiters, perfect service, splendid cuisine. Now I don't quite understand this part of the cure either, but the chef sends you a message that if you'd like him to make something special for you, he'll be glad to do so. Your husband orders pissaladiera, a special onion pie that he hasn't had since he was a boy in Nice. Your neighbor just takes the bill of fare: pâté de foie gras (well, it's liver cure, isn't it?), gnocchi romaine, fish, veal scallopini, salad, cheese, strawberry tart, and fruit. Wine, of course.

In the afternoon you sleep, or you go to a volcanic grotto in the side of a mountain and seat yourself, sheet-wrapped, on a bench in a cave with a lot of other phantoms of mixed sexes, and you sweat. No, I don't mean perspire. The heat is natural volcanic heat and so you sweat, torrentially. It's a very solemn matter, mixed volcanic sweating, and no distractions are allowed. You

keep your knees covered or you're spoken to by a mon-
itress, and you don't change places or the other phantoms glare at you and accuse you of creating a draft.

Then, in the evening, you feast on a dinner much
like your lunch, drink an espresso in the courtyard, and
fall into bed to recover for the early morning routine.

When the cure is over—it takes about thirteen
days—you feel splendid, you look rested, and the doctor
tells you your liver is now smaller and more supple. And
you go back to life in the capital until the year passes
and you are once more in need of the cure.

Well, of course, I went along with this whole performance the first year just to be a sport, but now I, too,
am responsible. I've grown a liver, I take good care of it,
I can't wait to go to Montecatini each year. I drink my
waters, bathe in strontium 90 and 7 Up, and wind up,
each time, with a liver "*Plus petit, moins dur.*" But every
now and then I get homesick for a stomach. And good
old American milk of magnesia.

La Place de la Discorde

4

I've said it before and I'll say it again: Paris traffic just isn't traffic at all. It's a chariot race and every driver thinks he's Ben Hur.

I have a California driver's license which I obtained in Los Angeles, and I don't care how high the death rate on the Los Angeles Speedway may be, I'll take it before the Place de la Concorde any day of the year. I can't very well take it *after* the Place de la Concorde because I'm not taking the Place at all. Nor the Étoile.

Not only because of the mortal danger, but because it is absolutely impossible for a foreigner to hold his end or anything else up in a traffic altercation there, or, for that matter, anywhere else in France. The French not only have it over you in fluency of tongue, but also in range and resourcefulness of insult and invective. Furthermore, because it is against the law to hit you, they've devised a series of menacing and hysterical gestures that will paralyze you much more effectively than a direct blow. Driving in France, and the conduct of the consequences thereof, is a deadly art.

To begin with, there's the matter of *style*. It takes a long time to catch on to that, and the best place to do it from is the side lines. The style of a Frenchman's behavior in a near-accident is entirely different from his style in a true accident. Of the two types of accident it is the first, the near-accident, which the foreigner should try to avoid. He stands a much better chance in a head-on collision.

Let's take an example: Two Frenchmen, each driving a Quatre Chevaux (that means Four Horses—what did I tell you: a chariot race), approach each other at a terrible speed from opposite directions in the Place de la Concorde. Just before the moment of truth, each jams on his brakes and the cars shriek to a stop, one centimeter apart. This is a serious situation. The drivers simultaneously emerge from their vehicles, slam their doors, and charge at each other until *they* are one centimeter apart. And what follows *then*! It isn't just the foaming mouths, the flailing arms, the bulging eyes and distended blood vessels, it's the things they say about your grandmother! And as for yourself, well—the things *you* are would stock a farmyard and overnourish the fields.

It is some curious sort of built-in electronic device in every Frenchman which determines the time limit of this kind of fray. Suddenly the opponents turn, march back to their cars, enter, slam the doors again, and then drive off screaming and shaking their fists until out of view. That, as I say, is the style of the near-accident.

Quite the contrary is the style of the full-scale holocaust. Take the same two Frenchmen in the same Quatre Chevaux. They approach each other at a terrible speed from opposite directions in the Place de la Concorde. This time they do not jam on the brakes and their cars do not shriek to a stop, but climb all over each other with a hideous crashing and crunching of metal and clinking of glass. As the last shard tinkles to the pavement, a silence falls. Then slowly there creep from the awful shambles the two drivers. They pull themselves upright, flick off the blood, and walk toward each other at a dignified and solemn pace. Twelve centimeters apart they stop and, swaying as little as possible, they discuss the accident in grave and courteous tones. Until the ambulance arrives. And the towing cars.

After that, I suppose, they send each other flowers. As I say, this is the only type of accident I can recommend to the visiting foreigner, if he *will* drive in France.

Now, of course, there's another aspect of the Frenchman in an automobile: the Frenchman in the role of questing Romeo. As long as a woman is *in* the car with a Frenchman she is completely safe, as the charioteer in him remains completely dominant and he is much more interested in overtaking the car in front of him than in overwhelming his companion.

But if you're *outside* the car, and he's in it, and he's moving and so are you, and you are both in the Bois (the Central Park of Paris), the huntsman in him will rise and suppress the charioteer, and all I can say is, I hope you're good at climbing trees!

When I left for France for the first time I was counseled, among other things, never to go shopping unchaperoned, that The Worst would happen to me if I did. Well, I took the advice very seriously, and so when necessity required that I venture out alone on the Champs Élysées soon after my arrival, I did so in fear and trembling. Down the avenue I walked and into the

Rue de Rivoli. Not an incident. Down the Rue Royale and into the Place de la Madeleine. Not a pass. Terror gave way to astonishment, astonishment to a sensation of letdown, letdown to indignation; finally I felt I had received a national insult.

Well, you can walk down any street in Paris in relative safety, but don't go near the Bois. If you do, within ten minutes ten cars will come slithering up to the curb and park just ahead of you. And when you sail past, ignoring them, they'll follow you around the block; and if you cut through the woods they'll block you at the other end. No, don't go promenading in the Bois unless you're with a large dog or you're on a tall horse. A camel would be even better!

All the French
speak French

5

Of course the thing that staggers you when you first come to France is the fact that all the French speak French—even the children. Many Americans and Britishers who visit the country never quite adjust to this, and the idea persists that the natives speak the language just to show off or be difficult. More than once Americans have arrived at my Paris house flushed and tardy, exclaiming that they were late because they had had the misfortune to get "one of those taxi drivers who *would* speak French!"

I must say that by the time I reached the Cannes Film Festival on my first trip to France, I was pretty well shaken myself. However, I rallied and decided to apply myself to learning the language. When I left the country two weeks later I was able to pronounce Keerque Dooglahce and Clarque Gobbluh with the best of them.

Then on my return in October I got down to business and started taking lessons three times a week with a professor, a textbook, and a notebook for my homework. I was encouraged by my professor to be brave and attempt not only words but phrases with taxicab drivers, news-vendors, anyone and everyone, and to cease depending on desperate gestures and strangled cries to make myself understood.

No point in practicing on Pierre—he was practicing on me, improving his English. So I started with the taxicab drivers. Fortunately for me they were always the kind who *would* speak French.

Of course, in the French cab, as in the Manhattan or Brooklyn cab, the driver always opens the conversation. And for the fare, in either case, the first principle is to understand what the driver has said. It really is more difficult in Paris. But one day after I'd started my lessons, a taxicab driver's opening gambit swam murkily into my consciousness and instead of just swimming out of it right away, it hesitated, stayed, and then miraculously separated itself into intelligible words, which, I gathered, had to do with Paris being pretty in the winter. I was thrilled and inspired, and instead of playing safe with my usual international "hmmm," suitable for all occasions, I assembled my first complete French sentence in less than 280 seconds and stated that I agreed, except for one thing: "Three days after it falls," said I, "the snow in Paris becomes very salty." That was one time a taxicab driver decided not to argue the point. And I still don't see why *salé* should mean salty when *sale* means dirty.

Not long after that, intoxicated by a really brilliant showing at my lesson, I gave some quite detailed instructions to another taxicab driver as to where I wanted

him to stop. This time I made a splendid *bouillabaisse* of *la crêpe* (pancake), *le crêpe* (widows' weeds), *arrêt* (stop), *arête* (fishbone), and rather authoritatively asked him to put me down at the fishbone of the autobus where the lady was standing wearing the pancake. He did, too.

Then there was the day I shook my professor. I'd been on a household shopping excursion and had been rather dismayed by the high cost of things. Well, I don't know if you see much difference between *matelot* and *matelas*, and I don't know how you'd complain about the price of a mattress. But anyway *I* rushed in to my professor at lesson time in a state of outrage and indignantly proclaimed that I had discovered that French sailors were *very* expensive!

I do better these days, but every now and then something will happen which makes it clear there's still room for improvement. A few months ago, for instance, I took my son, Benjamin, to see *Robin Hood* on the Champs Élysées. I made it years ago, when I was only sixteen to be inexact, and I was enchanted to find it running again in Paris after such a passage of time. Of course the film was dubbed with French voices and Maid Marian and Robin Hood and everyone else in Sherwood Forest were chattering marvelously away in the Gallic tongue. When the picture was over my son turned to me and said in his flawless French, "It was *for-mi-da-ble, for-mi-da-ble!* But, Mamma, you spoke better French *then* than you do now!"

And there was the evening not so long ago when I dined with a French publisher and his wife. After dinner, my hostess remarked on my accent, which, she observed, was "*très personnel.*" She said it wasn't typically American and it wasn't typically English. It was, she summed up, "*légèrement* Yugoslav"!

For dogs and children, of course, French is no problem at all. My Airedale, who came to France when he was fourteen, learned it in no time. We loved him very much and so he was a happy dog, although he had lost a leg in his early youth. As a matter of fact, his infirmity gave him a sort of distinction. I am sure he was the only bilingual, three-legged Airedale in existence.

And as for my son Ben, who was four when he settled down to live in France, he learned the language in six months and in two years won first prize in French in a French school. It just goes to show that we Americans *can* speak French if we just start early enough.

How is Ben's English? Lovely, simply lovely. He speaks it just like Charles Boyer!

No powder room
parade

6

One of the most striking anatomical differences between the French man and the French woman, and, indeed, between Americans generally and the French, is
the bladder. The male French bladder is unique and has
no relationship whatsoever to the female French bladder, which is even more remarkable and which is even,
one might say, admirable.

Coming from the land of the comfort station, I was
not really surprised to see, every few yards on every avenue in Paris, a curious circular metal screen, the use
of which I accurately guessed without having to ask.
But noting, for one cannot help noting it, that below
the screen, which always ends about two feet from the
ground, only trouser legs were visible, I discovered the
use was strictly limited to the needs of the male of
the race. The top of the screen, of course, is just above
head height, although an Englishwoman once claimed

to me that an exceptionally tall French friend of hers recognized her while he was engaged therein one day, and tipped his hat to her as she passed on the street.

The French male bladder is what you might call nervous. Not only are the metal screens placed for its convenience every few paces on every city street, but in the country, on the principal highways of France where no such contraptions exist, it is a frequent and quite ordinary thing to see a Frenchman stop his car, descend from it, and, not even bothering to seek a tree, get the matter over with. I have seen an entire family of males lined up on the roadside, all at the same time, getting the matter over with, while the ladies merely waited in the car. On the occasion of which I speak, there was a sort of protocol. Great-grandfather was closest to the road, so as not to have to walk too far; Grandfather was just beyond him and only just out of range; then came Father; then came Uncle Antoine, then Cousin Gaston; and little Paul was last of all. The most remarkable phenomenon of the entire practice is that the Frenchman manages this operation with such skill and finesse that never once have I seen the slightest indication of indecent exposure.

Now the French female bladder is exactly the contrary. It may not even exist at all. Not once has a Frenchwoman at lunch or dinner at my house, or even at my table in a restaurant, asked me where the ladies' room was. Having had a six-months course in a Notre Dame convent in Belmont, California (note that Notre Dame and Belmont are French words), I myself had had a certain training in this respect, and so I began to take the discreet rhythm of the female French bladder for granted as being just feminine. Then an ex-cover-girl friend of mine from California came to Paris and dined with my husband and me at the Berkeley. At the end of the meal, while we were drinking our coffee, my American friend stunned me by asking me the once-familiar but long-forgotten question as to the location of the Little Girls'. Well, frankly, I didn't know. However, wanting to be hospitable to my compatriot in a foreign land, I rose and accompanied her into the foyer in search, and every eye in the restaurant followed us with astonishment. The clientele thought we had quarreled with our husbands. All we were doing was engaging in the old American custom, the Powder Room Parade.

And I'm against it. I'm for an obligatory course in French feminine discretion and restraint. Let us teach it in the schools; let the Girl Scouts and Campfire Girls spread the word; let the women's clubs go into training. And the system *can* be taught. The daughter of Marie Antoinette and Louis XVI was only half French, and she learned it. Her German half made so perfect an adaptation that when she was brought back from the border after her parents' famous near-escape during the French Revolution, the deputy who accompanied her as a guard in her coach remarked with awe that during the twelve-hour nonstop ride, she did not manifest *"aucun besoin."*

I'm not surprised; but since *he* was a Frenchman, however did *he* manage???

The look
I left behind me

_____

7

In Hollywood a woman has "chic" if she wears a black velvet dress and a platinum anklet out to lunch, and she has "good taste" if she's always attired in a beige wool shirtmaker and a string of Saks Fifth Avenue pearls. But the most important look for her to have in dress is the "sexy look."

The sexy look starts with the toenails. They must be lacquered red, of course, and revealed, not concealed, by the shoe. The transparent plastic shoe was invented to meet this requirement of the sexy look. The really sexy plastic shoe has a four-inch heel of black suede or rhinestones, and with it must be worn sunset-colored nylons at five dollars a pair. Sheer. Expensively sheer.

The sexy dress begins just below the knee and is of a striking color and a glossy fabric. Satin, taffeta, moiré— any cloth which catches the light and *molds*. Design, cut, pleats, buttons, belts—details of any kind are of no concern; it's the outline that is underlined. The dress must cling to, sculpture, and emphasize the thighs, hips and waist, and stop at the sternum—in the front, I mean, not the back. And en route it must strain itself over an oversized bust. If the lady wearing the dress doesn't have an oversized bust, she must buy one.

Of course, when I arrived in France I found that the prevailing mode had nothing whatever to do with the look I left behind me. In fact, the sexy look had never been heard of. In France it's assumed that if you're a woman you *are* sexy, and you don't have to put a dress on to prove it, too.

The Paris principle seemed purest simplicity: if you *must* dress, then do it beautifully. No exaggerated protuberances, please. And if you're going to put a dress on, then don't create a deadly contest between it and whatever else you put on.

On the other hand, even in New York, where the best-dressed women of the U.S.A. buy and wear their clothes, the American woman, it seems to me, tries to rivet your attention to some complementary element of her costume. Let's face it, we're accessory crazy. We're conversation-piece mad. We must wear some item that will draw the eye—a bag, or a hat, or a brooch, or a bracelet. Something *original*. And we have a herd instinct about which item in any given year will be original. The result is very odd: an army of women all catching the eye with exactly the same eyecatcher.

Several years ago it was the oversized handbag or portable portmanteau. Black leather. Brass lock. Brass key. Two American friends of mine, fresh from New York, came to my Paris home at that time for an apéritif. Frightfully stylish types they were, and they could prove it: each carried the *original* accessory of the moment;

each had her large black satchel with the brass lock. Each valise caught my eye, all right, and held it there. Physically it was hard on me because the ladies were seated at different ends of the room. I've been a little walleyed ever since.

As I say, the principle in France is definitely anti-eyecatcher. It's the ensemble that counts, the harmonious look of the whole. And why wear a dress designed by a master if you're going to carry a trunk in front of it?

I must say, when you're home in the U.S.A. and you pick up the home-town paper after the first Paris collections have been shown in autumn or in spring, the view you get of what is going on over there is unnerving, to say the least. Invariably the paper carries a scare headline and under it, on the first page, a photo of a hat no one would be caught wearing on Halloween, to show what the giddy French are trying to put over this time. Well, it's a hat you won't see on any Paris street on All Hallows' Eve or on anybody else's Eve either. It's just something in or out of somebody's collection created expressly to give you a jovial sort of journalistic jolt.

Then there's that other journalistic ploy, the hemline hullabaloo. With each new collection the hemline seems to zoom up and down like a drunken elevator, but have you noticed that a really radical change in the hemline comes about once every five years and just about the time you *really* don't have a thing to wear?

There now, don't you feel better?

Oh, pouf!

8

Back home in Saratoga, California, and during the adolescent period of my life which might be designated B.C. or Before Cinema, I had been so thoroughly indoctrinated in the sober principles which governed the appearance of the young ladies of that admirable, attractive and conservative community, that even in the A.D. or After Damnation portion of my life, I still adhered to the belief that a girl should look as nearly as possible just the way the Lord made her.

This meant, in my case, that I made only the most elementary concessions toward make-up, limiting this form of embellishment to a thin film of face powder and a light application of rouge upon the lips. It also meant that a basic tenet of my personal religion was that the color of hair most suited to me was that with which I was born: God's color, or Deep Mouse.

After I went to Hollywood, no amount of persuasion

in the make-up and hairdressing dens of the City of Iniquity could cause me to yield so much as a single hair to so much as the most lightly tinted of rinses, or even, in fact, to anything other than five drops of lemon juice well mixed with rain water. Added to the influence of my basic training was, too, a horror of the kind of conjecture I had often overheard about other young female players, whose upbringing had very clearly not taken place in the Most Aristocratic Village in the Prune Belt.

I quailed when I heard it whispered about another ingénue: "It's a lovely color, but it isn't *hers*, you know" or "If you look at the roots, you can see for yourself" or "Why, the last time, they overdid it and it all fell *out*." There seemed to be a distinct implication in these suppositions that a girl who would dye her hair could not be other than false, through and through.

Then I came to France.

Now, not only was I still crowned with virgin tresses in their original, muted, dead-leaf tone, but, in addition, these locks were dressed in the purest style which the do-it-yourself-with-your-own-bobbypins method can achieve. For, although studio hairdressers had always done very well by me, I had never found a commercial hairdresser who would give me a coiffure inspiring anything in me but a headlong rush to my own bathroom and the salutary effect on the rigidity of my water-wave of my own comforting cold-water faucet.

When I first took up residence in Paris, I followed, of course, my long-established custom of the pure-soap-in-the-shower shampoo, the wind-it-around-your-own-finger-and-clamp-it-with-a-Sure-Grip set, and my walk-around-until-it-drips-dry mode of dehydration. The whole system gave me, I liked to believe, an enviable, trustworthy, limpid, natural look. And I was not mistaken. Which is why Pierre felt that a change was urgently required. If there is anything that appalls a Parisian, it is that crassly straightforward and sincere appearance which only a baby's bottom should have.

To the hairdresser's Pierre ordered me to go. To the best. And to go to the best was not a simple matter of calling up and making an appointment, but one of being correctly, formally, and personally introduced—sponsored, as it were, as used to be the case when it was still the custom to present young ladies at the Court of St. James's.

My sponsor once selected, the day came for her to take me in hand, make an appointment for me for the same time she made one for herself, and come to fetch me. Together we entered the sacred halls, mounted in the elevator to the floor where the Master himself presided, and then paused on the threshold of the Inner Sanctum, where only the elect might enter to receive the personal ministrations of the great Alexandre himself. His sanctum at that time was the smallest sanctum ever seen, and it was crowded to the sills and stuffed to the corners with the favored, among whom, that day, were two ambassadresses, seven countesses, one vicomtesse, four marquises, and no less than three royal princesses. I was the only commoner in the lot, and I should have cut and run had it not been for the fact that Pierre, with marvelous foresight, had picked as my sponsor a great Turkish beauty who, more than conveniently, happened to be *Son Altesse Royale*, the granddaughter of the last of the Sultans of All sultans. Cowering in her opulent shadow, I stood my ground.

Seven hours later I left the premises chastened, changed, but not at all disposed to head for the cold-water tap. I was moved, rather, to seek out one of those small wooden blocks the Japanese put under their necks at night in place of pillows. As I directed my course homeward I was careful to walk under the illuminating arc of the street lights, for not the least of the virtues of my new coiffure was its subtly altered hue. Alexandre had said God's color wouldn't do. It was now mink instead of muskrat.

Although the tone of my pelt is presently medium wild Labrador, it has undergone more than one mutation, all of which have been successful, with the exception of that which resulted on the dramatic day when it became my turn, as an established member of the royal court, to present my own eager candidate.

An American couple, with whom Pierre and I enjoyed a warm and devoted friendship, lunched with us one afternoon in the City of Light when they were en route from Italy to Le Havre on their way back to the United States. During the meal the female partner of the pair confided to me that she would like to go back home looking as if she had been to Paris. Would I, she wanted to know, act as her sponsor for an appointment with Alexandre? I would, and I did, and the next day, after she had had a shampoo in the monarchial washbasin, I led her personally into the Presence. Once she was established on the dais, I thought that a happy and exhilarating experience lay before her, but, alas, unaccustomed to royal usage as I myself once was, my friend committed the gravest possible breach of protocol. She told Alexandre how she wanted her hair to be done.

As is his way on such occasions, Alexandre instantaneously went into a trance, a trance which no human voice can penetrate, and taking up his scissors, he began to snip with smoldering precision at the lady's streaming

locks. She protested desperately but vainly that she had
not meant to have her hair cut, that she did not want to
have her hair cut, that she absolutely must not have her
hair cut. All she wanted was for it to be set and combed.
Alexandre's smoky eye showed not the faintest flicker
of understanding, and when he finally put his scissors
down and had murmured instructions to a lackey, my
friend was led, shorn and bleating piteously, to the
nether regions where, because it was the fashion of the
hour, the hair was treated to flecks of gold or silver.

I was there before her, and was horrified to see my
friend's pathetic little form, clad only in her slip and
hairdressing peignoir, swaying in the doorway as the
drops from her still streaming hair mingled with her
tears. Because there was one at hand, and in answer to
her supplications, I helped her to get the Hotel Bristol,
and subsequently her husband, on the telephone.

"Oh!" she cried when the marital voice came com-
fortingly on the line. "Something terrible's happened!"

"What?" exclaimed the husband with alarm.

"That dreadful man has cut me!"

"Who cut you?"

"Alexandre!"

"He cut you?"

"Yes, he cut me!"

"Where did he cut you?"

"He cut my hair! My hair! He's cut my hair!"

The distracted husband gave my friend immediate
and brisk instructions to pay the bill, call a cab, and
come back to the hotel exactly as she was. Down went
the receiver and off she started when my hand shot out
and grabbed her wrist.

With a tone I had never noted in my voice before nor

have I since, I heard myself saying, "Do you want to go home looking as if you had never been to Paris?"

"No," gasped my friend.

"Do you want to go home looking as if you *had* been to Paris?"

"Yes," she quavered.

"Then sit down," I thundered, "and do what I say. You are going to eat a sandwich, you are going to drink some tea, and you are going to see this thing through!"

Stunned by the voice of authority, soothed by the sandwich, and calmed by the tea, my friend docilely allowed the color specialist to do what he wished with her, and meekly she returned once more to the August One for the final operation. When it was all over, I took her to the Bristol in a cab, but the second she descended from it, I told the driver to gun the motor, and off I sped to sanctuary. My strength was gone. I could not face the husband.

That evening we were all expected at the same dinner party. It was at the Orangerie, now no longer in existence, and our host was another visiting American, Jack Warner. Pierre and I were at his table, I remember, together with, among others, Maurice Chevalier and Madame Arpels. Our friends were scheduled to sit at the immediately adjacent table and it was with considerable suspense that I awaited their arrival. However, when all the other guests were already seated, our couple still had not appeared. I was calling for more champagne when suddenly the door opened and in came our duo, radiant and serene. They smiled benignly at us, took their places, and aside from a murmur of interest over the newcomers, the party was as before.

I learned later that what had delayed our friends was

the minute examination before the mirror of every angle and every facet of the hairdress, and the coming of the decision "not to touch a single hair of it."

I was happy, of course, but with a pleasure not entirely unalloyed. In the confusion of the dramatic moments which had passed earlier in the coloring room, my tension had communicated itself to my own specialist, and, under his unsteadied and overlavish hand, my delicate shade of medium wild Labrador, lightly streaked with burnished gold, was not produced. I sat through that entire dinner party the perfect image of a ranch-bred chinchilla.

Since that perilous and suspenseful day, Alexandre has moved from his narrow sanctum to more palatial quarters further up the Rue du Faubourg St. Honoré, and the domain over which he now reigns is a series of ballrooms of which the first, the Blue Ballroom, is the throne room. Minor princes hold sway over the adjoining Rose Ballroom. The Green Ballroom is the ornamental torture chamber where, ranged around the walls, are those diabolic instruments, the *séchoirs*. The Yellow Assembly Room is devoted to the more amiable practices of shampooing and color work, and the Terre Cuite Lounge is given over to the art of the permanent.

The throne room is always crowded with court favorites, but a convenience has been provided them so as to keep the sills and corners disengaged and to avoid the risk of suffocation to sovereign and subject alike. It is a mammoth leopard-skin pouf, placed in the very center of the room so that the members of the court may rest and yet be ready to respond instantly to the royal summons. There, clustered upon it and grouped as if for a Winterhalter court painting, albeit in their socks and smocks instead of crinoline and *capeline*, are the ever-constant ambassadresses, baronesses, vicomtesses, countesses, marquises and royal princesses. Come to think of it, I'm surprised that pouf is clothed in leopard skin. It really should be ermine.

R.S.V.P.—if you dare

9

I suppose that after Paris traffic the biggest hazard which awaits the visiting American is the French social life.

To begin with, the bitter rumor which has reached your ears to the effect that the French can't stand foreigners and therefore will never receive you in their homes but merely in a restaurant, is a complete canard, as we say in American novels. In the first place, it's the French that the French can't stand, and in the second place, if they receive you in a French restaurant, who's complaining?

Now, the point is that the French *will* receive you in their homes, but only if they can do so in the style of Louis the Fourteenth. This means seventeen courses, and nine butlers behind every chair. Most important, it means a marvelous cook in the kitchen. And even in France marvelous cooks are a vanishing breed.

In other words, if you *are* invited to dine in a French

home, it means either that your hostess is gloriously at home on her range or that she's finally found a gem of a chef and wants to give a dinner party in a hurry, before she loses him.

If this last is your case, and you receive that engraved invitation, you are already in trouble. If you've managed to translate the French part of the invitation and are congratulating yourself on doing so, your eye at that moment will be struck by the single, ominous English word in the lower left-hand corner. It is the cryptic notation: SMOKING.

It paralyzes you. What can it possibly mean? Can it be true that the well-bred Gaul simply never smokes publicly in Paris and that you've been making your vulgar error in restaurants, taxicabs and hotel lobbies, when you should have been waiting for this private occasion when you are invited to dine and are given to know that at last, behind closed doors and in discreet and genial company, the privilege of smoking can finally be indulged in? No, surely that's not it. Then perhaps it means that you may not accept the invitation unless you are *willing* to smoke—that if you do accept you are not only expected but *required* to smoke. Oh no, it can't mean that, either. Then the sinister thought crosses your mind that a *special* kind of smoking is clearly implied. Marijuana? And bring your own, please? Or, possibly, opium. And damn well bring your own hookah.

The first time I received such an engraved invitation, before Pierre and I were married, I panicked. I called Pierre at his office and asked him weakly if he, himself, had found a similar one among his own mail. Yes, he had, to the same party, of course, since it was from friends of his to whom he'd introduced me.

"Well," I asked him, "what does 'smoking' mean? You know I've given up the habit, and I'd hate to break my vow, even for these charming people."

"Oh," he laughed, "that only refers to what one is supposed to wear!" And then he left the line.

Well, I sat down heavily after that remark, I can tell you. My word—"what one is supposed to wear"! What in the name of Heaven could a smoking costume possibly be, I wondered. Oh, how unsophisticated, how rudimentary we Americans are, I thought. Never, never have I had a smoking costume. Now, a smoking costume would be . . . well, for a man, anyway, it would be . . . one of those velvet jackets, perhaps, that Men of Distinction are always wearing in front of a fire with a glass of aged whiskey in hand and a pipe between the teeth? Or something made of plaid—didn't the Duke of Windsor wear something of the sort in a recent photo taken in a leisurely, smoking, evening moment? Or instead, perhaps a dressing gown of dark blue velvet, such as the one in which still other ads love to pose their genial cigar-smoking models? Yes, of course, this last was it, and Pierre was expected to attend in a really grand and luxurious *formal* dressing gown, and I was supposed to wear . . . There, I was hopelessly stuck. Not a negligee, surely. And I didn't have one, anyway.

Demoralized, I called Pierre again.

"I don't," I explained, "have anything to wear that is designed just for smoking. We wear any old thing for puffing away in our backward United States, you know."

"That reference is not to what *you* wear, just to what *I* wear," he replied. "You wear a dinner dress, of course," he continued, "and I wear smoking."

"What do you mean, you wear 'smoking'?" I asked.

"You know, 'smoking.' It's just the same sort of thing that men wear to a dinner party in the United States," he elucidated.

"You mean a dinner jacket?"

"Yes, yes, black tie—you know, 'smoking.'"

This time I hung up really full of bewilderment. Well, that beats all, I thought. In the States we think it's frightfully chic just to say "chic," and in France it's clear that a Frenchman just doesn't know his way around if he doesn't flash his knowledge of English terms and usages. Black tie, no. Smoking, yes.

Well, once you get over this first perilous hurdle, you are in for others, and they are usually compounded if you should be invited to the very richest type of Parisian establishment. This, though in the French manner, will not be French, but South American. Don't believe it when they tell you that the Greeks are the richest people in the world. It's not true. The very, very richest are the South Americans. And when they live in France they do things as the French do. Pure Louis the Fourteenth. And they *always* have a marvelous cook.

All right, you've got the "smoking" thing settled, you dress in your best dinner gown and you get into a taxi with your escort and head for the address on the card of invitation. It is probably on the Avenue Foch. Sumptuous. What follows then will be something like what happened to me one night when I set off with Pierre for one of my first grand soirees.

We entered the foyer of a magnificent and luxurious apartment. Someone took my wrap. We proceeded to the salon. At the entrance were our hostess, our host, and an extremely handsome woman with blue eyes and auburn hair, wearing a yellow velvet Dior gown. Beyond them other guests stood talking, and smoking, I noticed with a certain relief, perfectly ordinary cigarettes. We greeted our hostess, our host, and were presented to the charming lady in yellow. She was, so I understood, the Comtesse de Paris. She shook hands with me graciously and then gave her hand to Pierre. To my astonishment, his heels seemed to snap together and suddenly he bent double. At first I thought he'd suffered a cramp, but then I realized that he had actually *bowed*, deeply, over the Comtesse's hand. When we were at a discreet distance I turned on him for an explanation—he who had never, never kissed mine, had never so much as nodded over it, either, much less done a jackknife at the very sight of it. The Comtesse de Paris, he told me, would be Queen of France if France were a monarchy, and it is the custom to accord her the courtesies which are traditionally hers.

I thought that over, and democrat though I am, loyal citizen of a republic though I be, I had to admit that this reasoning of the modern Republican French was very nice indeed. Very attractive, very sensitive. Just as it should be. I then turned to other guests and began to converse.

Now, the guest of honor on this particular occasion was a fellow American. None other than Fleur Cowles, in fact. But minutes went by and she'd not arrived. Couriers eventually brought news to the hostess that a grave misadventure had befallen Fleur at the Ritz. She was locked in the bathroom and could not get out. However, the entire repair force of the hotel was working on the situation and messages assured the hostess that the crews of carpenters, plumbers, and locksmiths would be able to release her at any moment from her sarcophagus. Eventually, I noticed a quickening of the atmosphere, a sudden new radiance in the room, and looking toward the entrance of the salon I saw Fleur, dazzling in tur-

quoise lace, greet her host and hostess. She then passed
to the Comtesse de Paris and promptly fell to the floor.
However, she recovered with extraordinary rapidity and
marvelous grace and carried on, as did everyone near
her, with the most astonishing aplomb, as if nothing un-
toward had occurred.

Then with a sensation as of a thousand elevators
plunging at five hundred miles an hour down through
the hollow void of my interior, I realized what Fleur had
done. She had *curtsied*. Curtsied! And no doubt about
it, every single one of the ladies in the room must have
done the same thing. Every single one except one. Me.

I will never, never get over it. The cold, hideous realization that I'd let down my country, that in front of
the French, the South Americans, the multi-nationed
guests, I, and I alone, had failed to render the cour-
tesy that was expected of me was enough to embalm
me on the spot for *my* sarcophagus. Somehow I pulled
myself together and determined to make a brave face
throughout the rest of the evening, although it loomed
before me an endless, accusing witness of my appalling
disgrace.

When we entered the baronial dining hall and were
seated at the long, magnificent table, I began to feel a
little better, although I was placed really perilously close
to the Comtesse de Paris. She was, in fact, in the position of honor directly opposite her host, on her immediate right was a French general who looked exactly like
Charles Boyer, and immediately next to him, alas, was
me. I mean I.

However, as each splendid course was served, and as
each appropriate wine glass among the series before my
place was filled by a footman at my right, I did really

begin to feel a little bit at ease. I talked to my neighbors and listened with grave, responsive attention to everything the Comtesse said. Just as I was willing to live again, a most appalling thing happened.

Suddenly, on my left, between the general and me, a white-gloved hand thrust a silver tray. On it was a single, huge, bulbous sort of crystal vase. In the vase was a deep red liquid. And at this moment, somewhere above my head, a stentorian voice rang out with some sort of sonorous pronouncement. It seemed to me that a hush fell upon the table and that every eye was observing me. I looked at that white-gloved hand, at that silver tray, at that curious curving vase like a giant brandy snifter, and wondered what I could possibly be expected to do about it. As the minutes ticked by it occurred to me that I was just supposed to admire it. So I did. The hand, the tray, the glass, remained. Then I thought perhaps I was supposed to sniff, so I did. The hand, the tray, the glass, remained. Desperately, wildly, I looked up and gasped, "*Merci*," just to indicate to the bewigged and begloved gentleman that I'd already received the very maximum of pleasure from admiring and sniffing and that he could now take the tray and the glass on, on, on—anywhere at all. Mercifully, the hand, the tray, the glass, were finally withdrawn. I watched them, fascinated, as they rounded the table and were presented to the lady across from me. She simply took the glass and placed it beyond her plate. A second later she sipped from it.

This time I really did want to die. There was no longer any point in living. I would have died right then and there, too, except that I realized it would be the summit of my gaucheries if I did so.

I turned to my general, and because of his nice,

warm Charles Boyer eye, I said, "You know, I really am an American in Paris. When that enormous glass was presented to me I simply could not imagine what it was for. I'd never seen one before in all my life."

He smiled, and then made of me a friend forever. He said, "Now that you know, would you like another one just like it?"

He signaled the footman to bring me another glass exactly like the one I'd so recently refused. This time I took it and did just what I'd seen the lady opposite me do. It isn't often that you get a second chance in life, and that French general made me feel I'd never messed up the first one.

When the sumptuous repast was over, and we were all in the salon once again, I felt so much better that I really did have a rather wonderful time. You couldn't say I was reincarnated, but I was, at least, revivified.

Then, as if she'd forgiven me for my two fiascos, who should come over to me, as the evening wore on, but the radiant and gracious Comtesse de Paris. She said that she understood that I was soon to marry a Frenchman, and that she not only wished me happiness in my marriage, but also in my new life in France. I was deeply touched by her gesture, and as we shook hands and said good night, I felt that at last I'd been fully redeemed. I followed her with grateful, misty eyes as she passed from guest to guest. Then I saw, with horror, one lady after another drop to the floor in a deep, graceful, nobly executed curtsy of adieu.

Well, since then, I've been practicing and I've done quite nicely, thank you, by the King and Queen of Greece, the Duke and Duchess of Windsor, and Princess Alice of England. I've been on the alert, too, and only the other day I was brilliantly ready. I met Alexander of Yugoslavia in the Rue Pierre Charron, and I want you to know that when our hands met I made a beautiful, first-class, distinguished knee bender. I do wish, though, he'd not been on the sidewalk and I'd not been crossing the street at the time. Why, oh, why did we have to meet just as I reached the gutter?

*The time, the money
and the energy*

IO

The first time I flew back to California to make a film
after my marriage, I received, on the day of my arrival in Hollywood, an invitation from some very good
friends of Pierre's and mine to spend my first evening
with them at dinner, together with other mutual friends
whom they'd asked to join them. It was a delightful and
joyful reunion for me with people I'd not seen for some
time. In the gaiety of the moment, although it was four
in the morning in Paris, my host decided to telephone
Pierre, and placed a call by the transatlantic cable,
which would assure clear and perfect communication.

While we were all at the table, I heard the telephone
ring, and a few moments later the butler came into the
dining room and whispered into my host's ear. Since I
was directly on his left and have 20-20 hearing, I heard
the butler state, "The operator says she's been ringing

the Paris number for ten minutes and there's no response."

"Tell her to try again in an hour," replied my host, a look of panic spreading over his face. Then, since he was a very successful studio executive, experienced at meeting every sort of disastrous crisis, an expression of confident geniality quickly replaced the panic, and he announced to us all that the cable was not yet free and that the operator had not yet been able to reach Paris.

I knew exactly what my American host was thinking: *That French devil, the first night his wife's away, he's out on the town.* Knowing perfectly well that that French devil, the first night his wife was away, was spread-eagled and unconscious all over our double bed, darn glad to have it to himself, I observed that I was sure there'd be no response until midnight California time, nine in the morning Paris time, when the maître d'hôtel would come into the kitchen to heat the croissants. Since we'd just installed ourselves in a house with only one phone, which was on the first floor, and since my husband was asleep on the second floor and the domestics on the third, no one would hear that phone until they were awake and perpendicular. A flicker of tender pity gleamed in my friend's eye, and I realized that the more I might say, the more pathetic my case would appear to him. I was not only the betrayed wife, I was the duped wife.

Well, since I was myself still geared to Paris time, I'd been up without sleep about twenty-four hours, and when 11 P.M. California time came around, much as I wanted to talk to Pierre as he crunched his croissants, I reeled off to bed at the Beverly Hills Hotel. At my host's house, however, my husband was on the line at midnight (9 A.M. in Paris), choking on his croissants, furious that his wife hadn't remained to talk to him and, forgetting the difference in time, furious that I'd been up until eight in the morning. Darkly suspicious he was. My first night back in the States and I'd been carousing about until dawn rose simultaneously over Montmartre and Mount Wilson.

I must say that I understood my host's apprehension and misapprehension very well indeed, because before I learned better I too thought, as most Americans do, that infidelity is as common to the French husband as *café complet.*

I remember that during my first weeks as a newly engaged, new resident of Paris, I received from a malevolent Irishman a copy of Nancy Mitford's *The Blessing*, which concerns an Englishwoman who marries a Frenchman and discovers that, although he obliges her beautifully in the evenings, he spends his afternoons with his mistress. The book shook me. At each fresh example of the husband's perfidy, I exclaimed to Pierre: "So *this* is the way a Frenchman spends his honeymoon!" "Is *this* the way a French husband toys with the tea hour?" "Is *this* . . . , etc."

Pierre was enraged. Finally he threatened to throw the book out the window, howling, "*No*, eet ees *not* true about Gaston, Alain, Georges, Robert, Raymond, Thierry, Jean-Pierre, Jean-Claude, or Jean-Paul!" Then he ran out of breath. I was enheartened, but not wholly convinced. So I studied all our friends—Gaston, Alain, Georges, Robert, Raymond, Thierry, and all three Jeans—and found that it was clearly true, none of them was unfaithful to his wife, and obviously had no desire ever to be so.

Somewhat reassured though I was about my own personal destiny, I felt a curious sensation of dismay and bewilderment about Frenchmen as a whole, and confided to André Maurois one day at tea that I was rather shocked by the discrepancy between the reputation of the French husband and the low incidence of infidelity that really existed *chez lui.*

Having agreed that the average Frenchman much preferred to be faithful to his wife, Maurois reflected for a moment and decided that the reputation must once have been well-founded—"in the romantic period," he said, "over a century ago, when the life of the feelings was given so much importance, and when the poetic imagination was accorded so much expression. Nowadays the style is different because conditions are different. The French husband no longer has the leisure that his inheritance used to assure him, because the last two wars have wiped out the old French institution of the carefully nurtured and passed-on family fortune, and almost every modern Frenchman must therefore work. He marries young and has his children promptly. And you know," concluded Maurois, "to have a mistress, a man must have the money for it—and the time—and the energy!"

With Pierre that evening I did a little careful checking. The family fortune had been thoroughly wiped out by 1946. He must have been bewildered by my expression of pure delight. He was puzzled but pleased when I myself took *The Blessing* and threw it out the window. After all, it was about the rarest type of modern Frenchman—a marquis, who had the time, the money, and the energy!

My French blue
eyedrops

11

Another thing about which I'd had no instruction before I landed at Orly for the first time was French medicine. It's a world of its own. When I got off the plane on that initial visit I did so with my own bottle of paregoric, manufactured in the United States, clutched in my hand. This was for the disaster which my friends at home had said would follow if I should have the misfortune to drink the tap water. It came in handy because, although I didn't drink the water, I did brush my teeth with it. Anyway, the point is, I brought with me Stateside paregoric. I also brought with me American aspirin, American mercurochrome and American Band-Aids. I wasn't going to trust the French products, even if they happened to have such articles, which I very much doubted.

And I felt the same way when I disembarked the second time, to make my home permanently in France. However, one day, coming back to Paris from Nice, I got a cinder in my eye, and nothing I did for that eye made it any better. It grew horribly inflamed. Eyelids, upper and lower, were bloated red, and the eyeball itself was hideously crisscrossed with scarlet veins. I'd developed conjunctivitis.

There was nothing to do but call a French doctor. He prescribed blue eyedrops. I'd never seen anything like them before, and I knew they'd blind me. But the conjunctivitis was going to do that anyway, and to hurry up my inescapable fate and get it over with, I used the eyedrops.

When the blue of those drops met the red of my eyes, the effect was dramatic. By dyeing the whole eyeball blue they gave me the illusion for a good ten minutes that I'd been instantaneously cured of the disease. And they were soothing. They were wonderful. In the end they did cure the conjunctivitis, and even now, whenever my eyes are the slightest bit inflamed, I use them with perfect confidence. Next time you see me in a color film, and remark the fresh tint of the whites of my eyes, it's not the good, clean life I lead, it's my French blue eyedrops.

Well, this experience gave me courage, and I went on to discover and try other French medicines. I found that for every complaint known to man, and for the extra ones known only to the French, there is an armory of medicines of all sorts, colors, and consistencies. For anything you care to mention, and for anything you don't care to mention, there are powders, effervescent pastilles, capsules, pills, salves, ointments, lotions, injections, inhalations, sprays, drops, and suppositories.

And king among them all is the last-mentioned, the suppository.

When I was making *Proud Rebel* in the States not so long ago, I met Margo, the great Mexican actress, who'd recently come back from a visit to France, and she told me her story about just this.

She'd fallen sick in Paris with the worst, the very worst sore throat of her life. Friends called a French doctor and he examined her thoroughly. At the end of the examination, he remarked that indeed her throat was severely inflamed, but he was sure she would find a marked improvement after a day or two of taking the medication he was going to prescribe for her: a suppository. She accepted this statement calmly but could not refrain from saying, "Doctor, I know that there are many things about which we Americans are ignorant, but would you be kind enough to tell me just why, why, when my affliction is in the *throat*, you have prescribed a suppository?"

"Because," replied he, "here in France we administer any number of different medicines for all sorts of illnesses in this manner. For two reasons: first, given this way, the medicine reaches the blood stream more rapidly than when given orally; second, in bypassing the upper organs, it does not disturb the liver."

Margo was staggered. "Doctor," said she, "this is the soundest, most sensible, most remarkable theory I have ever heard of in the field of medicine. Now will you please tell me why we in the United States have not adopted the practice?"

"Madame," replied he, "it is a Protestant country."

Sometimes, when I'm filming, I become over-anxious about sleeping, because sleep is so important for

an actress and the quality of her work. Consequently I
work myself into such a state of worrying about whether
I will or I won't sleep, that I don't.

About to start a film in England and Spain in 1954,
I confided my problem to my doctor in Paris, and he
prescribed for me a mild sleeping drug, administered,
of course, in what I had grown to accept as the classic
manner, reaching the blood stream in nothing flat and
bypassing the upper organs.

It worked beautifully, and I went from England to
Spain perfectly tranquil, knowing I would awaken fresh
every morning after a good night's sleep during which
my liver had been in no way disturbed.

One week we had a series of night shots to do. This
means suddenly going to work when the sun goes down
and going to bed when the sun comes up. The second
part sounds easy, I know, but just try making a profes-
sion out of it. Anyway, this time I wasn't worried, I was
prepared. However, after the first night's work, a black-
bearded, six-foot-seven Englishman in the cast was desperate. He just knew he wouldn't sleep a wink all day,
and the second night's work, for which all his most perilous dueling scenes had been scheduled, loomed before
him, heavy with hideous possibilities. He was sure he'd
end that second night skewered. Forthwith, of course, I
told him I had a perfectly marvelous sleeping preparation which would guarantee him ten full hours of total
repose, and I'd be happy to send a cylinder to his room
in an envelope.

He was illuminated with joy and relief. In parting,
I explained to him that it was a *French* sleeping prepa-
ration, if he understood my meaning. That evening
I reported to the set and found my Englishman there

before me. He came over to my side and said, "I say, it was jolly decent of you to have sent me that sleeping preparation, but you know, it was awfully hard to get down."

"Get down," I exclaimed aghast.

"Yes, really quite difficult, don't you know. But I finally rolled it into a ball and chased it down with a glass of water."

"And then what happened?" I gasped.

"Oh, in ten minutes I was out like a light," he replied. "And for twelve hours at that."

For a man whose upper organs had not been by-passed, he looked very well indeed.

Now here I would like to put in a word for the French remedy employed on the very rare occasions when, instead of a liver attack, a case of simple stomach ache has definitely been established. This splendid cure consists of the practice of eating charcoal. Granulated charcoal. It comes in a red tin, looks like what lines any ordinary chimney flue, and a single spoonful of this marvelous stuff, followed by a swallow of water, will really do wonders for a common cramp. Additionally, it has the highly desirable characteristic of dyeing your tongue jet-black. You go around for hours with the identifying mark of a purebred chow.

And as to the French doctor's general examination and checkup, buy your round-trip ticket now. It's more than worth the price. Here's my own personal experience:

A year or so ago I seemed to be in a sort of rundown condition, inexplicably tired and mysteriously listless. Pierre made an appointment for me with one of the most celebrated general practitioners of the city, and the day came for my checkup.

The doctor went over me very thoroughly indeed, and as he completed the first phase of the examination he remarked, "Madame, you have a magnificent organism!"

I must say, I immediately felt considerably stronger right then and there.

Then he asked me to stand while he took my blood pressure, and then sit down while he repeated the procedure. After I had completed this simple operation he continued, "However, Madame, you have low blood pressure—"

I was dismayed.

Quickly, the doctor reassured me by saying, "—which has a certain advantage. It means you will absolutely never die of high blood pressure."

I was delighted.

"Nevertheless, Madame," he went on, "it also means that whenever you stand up, your blood pressure goes down. And whenever you sit down, your blood pressure goes up."

I was baffled.

"And therefore, Madame," he summed up, "you will always be at your best while lying down."

I was overcome.

"The treatment I prescribe to correct the condition," he resumed—

I was recalcitrant.

"—is: *les exercises violentes!*"

I was breathless.

"*Surtout*, Madame, above all, Madame, *le ski et le tennis.*"

I was chagrined.

However, sport that I am, I rushed right up to Switzerland and, because it was midwinter and 20 degrees Fahrenheit, I started taking lessons at once in

le ski. And do you know, that French doctor was absolutely right? As all who witnessed my prowess on those
snowy and much abused slopes will testify, I was unquestionably and consistently at my very, very best
while lying down.

The great Centigrade-Fahrenheit debate

12

Shortly after Ben and I had come to France to live and were settled in our apartment near the Étoile, Ben came down with a fever, runny nose, cough and earache. It was near Christmastime and Pierre had left Paris for Nice to visit his mother, who was, herself, in very fragile health. I found myself, therefore, alone in the foreign capital with a sick child and only six weeks of French lessons under my hatband.

Fortunately, I had met the Canadian wife of one of the directors of a major French newspaper, and through her I obtained the name of a child specialist who could speak a little English. I called him, very anxious indeed, described Ben's symptoms, and told him that he had a temperature of 102.2 degrees. "How much is that," asked he, "in Centigrade?" Naturally, I'd had no idea that he was going to turn our conversation into a chemistry quiz and had not prepared myself for this eventuality.

I replied, of course, that I didn't know—and wondered if in France the prerequisite for a visit by a pediatrician was that the mother pass some sort of advanced studies examination. I had certainly flunked the test.

Although I had not expected the French to have aspirin, Mercurochrome, Band-Aids, and the like, I did, on arriving in France, expect them to have feet, miles, pounds and Fahrenheit. In this last instance, as in the first, I was very much mistaken. They do not have feet (oh, they have the kind you walk on, all right, but not the other sort—you know what I mean), nor do they have miles, pounds or Fahrenheit. Instead, they have centimeters, kilometers, kilograms and, alas, Centigrade.

Now, it had been a long time since I had done my chemistry studies, but it had been even longer since the doctor had done his, and although I did not know how much 102.2 was in Centigrade, neither, of course, did he. And he was not disposed to come to see Ben until he did. His advice to me was to send someone out to buy a French thermometer, take Ben's temperature anew, and telephone him again. I did as he asked me to, and when the French thermometer arrived at the door, I took it, washed it off with some American alcohol which, naturally, I'd had the foresight to bring with me from the States, and popped it into Ben's mouth. After letting it have a good cook in his oven, I drew it out, looked at it, and nearly fainted. It registered 39.

I thought Benjamin must have gone into severe shock. But no, as the room stopped circling and my eyes uncrossed, I perceived that he was perfectly conscious and as rosy as a peach. With a certain embarrassment I phoned the doctor again to say that I had followed his instructions and that Ben, after all, had a temperature of a mere 39. The doctor said that I mustn't be concerned about Ben's fever being so high, but that he would be right over. The conversation was pure surrealism. So were the days that followed, as Ben's temperature moved up to 39.3, upward again to 39.5, down to 38.2, and finally settled at a figure which seemed to me to be ominously low, 37.0. Five points above freezing, in my lexicon.

What made the situation really desperate was that my American thermometer, in the general excitement and out of sheer resentfulness, no doubt, had thrown itself off Ben's bedside table in a suicide leap and smashed itself to bits. Consequently, I now had no point of reference whatever. And I knew it was hopeless to turn the tables on the doctor and ask him how much 38.2 was in Fahrenheit.

However, Ben regained his strength rapidly and, finally, when he was, at last, perfectly well, I decided that it would be quite all right for me to leave him for a few days while I left town to recover from the general strain. I put him in the hands of a French nurse who adored him and held him in thrall at the breakfast table by saying, "Let's pretend we are lovers," a custom which did, I admit, give me a slight qualm; but, deciding that at the age of four this type of talk does not really risk being too debilitating, I went off to Chamonix in the upper Alps to regain my equilibrium. I must say that a mountain peak is not the best place to seek one's balance, but at least the air is bracing for the nerves.

In Chamonix I brooded over the new, real, and apparently to be perpetual, threat to my peace of mind: the unholy mystery of the centigrade thermometer. I had learned that whereas one degree above normal

Fahrenheit, or 99.6, was hardly something to inspire a rush for the oxygen tent, nevertheless, one degree above normal Centigrade, or 38 instead of 37, did require a modicum of care. Bed, in fact, and at least a thorough survey of symptoms and a report to the doctor. And whereas five degrees above normal Fahrenheit, or 103.6, was very serious but never fatal, five degrees above normal Centigrade, or 42, was something only horses ever survived.

Beyond this, I was in darkest ignorance and total bafflement. Then, on my second day in Chamonix, I met the two great mountaineers Lachenal and Terray, the second of whom was soon to scale Mount Annapurna, at 27,000 feet, in the Himalayas (no, I don't know how much that is in meters, and don't ask me). Well, it struck me that these men might know how to figure Centigrade into Fahrenheit and vice versa, so I asked them. They did not know. However, they did know one fact, and I can quite see how they *would* know it in the chill of those upper altitudes; they said that 40 degrees below zero Centigrade was exactly as cold as 40 degrees below zero Fahrenheit. I remarked to myself, as Benjamin, recently introduced to Sherlock Holmes, would say, "Ah, the missing clue!"

And it was, too. I stayed in bed in my room for twenty-four hours straight with a clutch of pencils and a quire of paper and my one tantalizing fact to chew over, and I scribbled and scribbled and figured and figured and multiplied and divided and added and subtracted. And finally, triumphantly, I found a formula which would translate Centigrade into Fahrenheit. Naturally, I rushed right out to find Lachenal and Terray and, locating them, I gave them the great news. They did not seem to be as excited as they should have been. They were interested, but not elated. I suppose if you are planning to climb the second highest mountain in the world you get blasé about some things. Anyway I, personally, had no doubts in my mind as to which was the greater accomplishment. Try climbing Mount Annapurna and doing what I did, and tell me honestly which is really the more difficult.

Returning to Paris, I pondered for the next year over the predicament of all the other American mothers in France who were going through the same bewilderment which I had gone through, and of all the mothers who descend upon Europe during the tourist season, totally unaware of what lies before them in mystification and torturing perplexity. And I finally decided that it was my patriotic duty to impart to my fellow countrywomen my marvelous find. There was only one way I could do it: by means of the letters column, called "From the Mailbag," of the Paris edition of the *New York Herald Tribune*. I thereupon wrote the following epistle which appeared in the aforesaid column thus, and under the following heading:

Formula

I have devised a formula for transposing temperature readings from Centigrade to Fahrenheit.

I cannot say it is a simple method, but as a mother once distracted by the incomprehensible readings of my child's Centigrade thermometer during his first illness in France, I can say that it is better than none.

This is the method:

Multiply the Centigrade reading by 1.8 and add 32.

Here is an example of the accuracy of the system:

1. A "normal" temperature reading Centigrade is 37 degrees.
2. A "normal" temperature reading Fahrenheit is 98.6 degrees.
3. 37 x 1.8 = 66.6
4. 66.6 + 32 = 98.6!

Last year at Chamonix I had the pleasure of meeting Lachenal and Terray, of the Annapurna Expedition, and when I asked Terray if he understood the mysteries of the two systems of heat measurement, he replied that he was certain they had one thing in common: they were identical at 40 degrees below zero. I began from there and evolved the above method, which, if it does nothing else, may inspire someone to come forward with a simpler one, thereby contributing to the peace of mind of the American mother during her first season in France.

> *Olivia de Havilland*
> *Paris, February 26, 1955*

Do you follow me? Take out a pencil and try it.

A few days later, the following letter appeared in the same letters column:

From Centigrade to . . .

To the *New York Herald Tribune:*

May I contribute to the peace of mind of an American mother in Paris by suggesting to Miss de Havilland of today's letters column that a simple and easy-to-follow formula for converting temperature readings from Centigrade to Fahrenheit may be found in almost any elementary high school or chemistry text.

The formula she has so admirably devised (1.8 Centigrade plus 32 equals Fahrenheit) is, I regret to say, not original. I learned the same one some few years ago in pharmacy school. It was not new then.

Another formula, equally simple, and perhaps preferred by minds unaccustomed to the decimal system, is the following: for the Fahrenheit equivalent, multiply the Centigrade reading by $9/5$ and add 32. Frequently, it is possible to convert with this formula without using pen and paper. (Conversely, it is F minus 32 times $1/9$ equals C.)

One other formula eliminates the 32 entirely: take Centigrade reading, add 40, multiply by $9/5$, subtract 40. *Voilà!*

In this instance, however, I fail to see any need for conversion; "normal" temperature is 37 degrees Centigrade. An alarming variation in Fahrenheit, it seems, should be alarming in Centigrade.

I would suggest to other Americans faced with a similar problem, that they dispense with all formulas and purchase a new thermometer, one calibrated in degrees Fahrenheit.

Clarence R. Currie
S/Sgt. USAF
Manston, England, March 2, 1955

For a girl who started this adventure from 40 degrees below zero both Centigrade and Fahrenheit, I have a very hot temper. In a flash, after reading Sergeant Cur-

rie's comments, I was at the boiling point: 100 degrees
Centigrade, 212 Fahrenheit. Consequently, I sat down
and shot off a tart reply to the sergeant via the Mailbag.
It was printed thus:

International Fever

To the *New York Herald Tribune:*

    If I were Staff Sergeant Currie I think I would
take *my* temperature!

    Yours for more available pharmaceutical books,
and French doctors who know what you mean when
you say your child has a temperature of 102.8!

Olivia de Havilland
Paris, March 5, 1955

Although Sergeant Currie was apparently never
heard from again, a great many other people were. A
flood of missives engulfed the letters column and among
them were the following:

Kilos to Pounds

To the *New York Herald Tribune:*

    The things that go on in this world! The last
time I was in Hollywood, Olivia de Havilland was
a glamour girl and the only figures (ahem) she was
interested in had to do with, well, you know. Now
she's "an American mother" and worried about
translating Centigrade into Fahrenheit and the mul-
tiplication table. With fractions yet. Wow! Does the
Hays office know about this, 'Livvy? Do they ap-
prove? Isn't this the sort of activity likely to lower
the stock of the American glamour biz?

Ah, well, since we're on the subject—and since I'm not an American mother but a mere American male—something else lies closer to my selfish heart. How in the name of all that is hectic do you translate kilos into pounds? I would like to find out whether all this good French cooking is adding to my poundage. Or is it better not to know?

Wolfe Kaufman
Paris, March 2, 1955

That Clear Now?

To the *New York Herald Tribune:*

What's all this hullabaloo about Fahrenheit and Centigrade? Any schoolchild knows that 32 Fahrenheit is equal to zero Centigrade, so if you add 18 to 32, which makes 50, and put it above 32 Fahrenheit and add 10 to zero Centigrade and put it above zero Centigrade you have 50 Fahrenheit is equal to ten Centigrade and so on up, and you subtract under 32 Fahrenheit and zero Centigrade.

An American in Cannes
Cannes, March 5, 1955

Knew It Already

To the *New York Herald Tribune:*

Sorry, Miss de Havilland did not *devise* any formula at all; the formula for transposing Centigrade temperature readings into Fahrenheit as quoted by Miss de Havilland has been used by the undersigned for at least twenty-five years! . . .

S. H. Newman
Paris, March 2, 1955

By this time, of course, I was living exclusively for the letters column of the *New York Herald Tribune*. A state of affairs which could not be permitted to continue, in case Benjamin should get the sniffles again and need me to take his temperature and to figure the whole thing out by you-know-what. Therefore, to tie the matter off, I wrote a third letter to the *Tribune*, which promptly appeared in the usual place, with a heading which gratified me deeply. I do think it was nice of them to refer to you-know-what as "The."

The Formula

To the *New York Herald Tribune:*

Well, if my letter did nothing else, it certainly inspired others to come forward and contribute to the peace of mind of *this* American mother!

Mathematics not being my strong point, when I devised (I beg your pardon, stumbled upon) the formula about which I wrote you, I always had the uneasy feeling that there must be a flaw in it somewhere. However, we now have the assurance (and from all sides, too) that it is a classic formula and can be used with perfect confidence.

With my thanks to your contributors,

Yours for the tried and true,
Olivia de Havilland

On the same day that this article of correspondence made its appearance in the Mailbag, I went to lunch at Mrs. Biddle's house on the Left Bank. A lot of guests were standing about and chatting in the background as I entered the drawing room and found my hostess posted just within the doorway. She greeted me, and then said, indicating the gentleman to whom she'd just been talking. "I'd like you to meet Eric Hawkins—the editor of the *Herald Tribune*."

As he leaned forward over the small table which stood between us, I detected not only a twinkle in Mr. Hawkins' eye, but also a flash of reflected light just below my direct line of vision. Just under our clasping hands, I then saw, on the table, a very essential article indeed. It was a small column of glass mounted on a frame; up the column ran the red line of a magic fluid, and on each side of the column were printed small numerical figures, one side headed by the initial *C*, and the other side headed by the initial *F*. Of course, none of us contributors had thought of *that* solution. But just to be sure that the Centigrade-Fahrenheit thermometer-in-one was doing its job, I gave it a thorough check. It was accurate. By the Formula, it proved out.

Where do you keep
your bathtub?

13

All this time that you've been having your housing problems back in the United States, I've been having mine, here in France.

When I planted that pennant on the Left Bank in October of 1953, I did so behind the Palais Bourbon, the classical eighteenth-century building which was once the abode of a Royal Duchess and is now the arena of the Republic's National Assembly—that is to say, the French House of Representatives.

Just off the Palais' Place, some friends of Pierre's had found Ben and me a little apartment, and when I first saw its small, intimate, low-ceilinged rooms, I was utterly enchanted with them. They had recently been freshened with paint and paper and provided with more than one piece of furniture in what was to me then the graceful but still foreign and unfamiliar style of Louis the Fifteenth.

Of course, the entry did serve as sitting room and dining room as well as coat, boot, and umbrella catcher, but beyond it was a charming, single-purpose bedroom for me, and adjoining mine, a bedroom for Ben, hung most attractively, though not exactly boyishly, in opulent red damask. As we installed ourselves, I heard the great clock of the Palais sounding out sonorously and musically, and to my Western, American ears it seemed to be the very voice of Old Europe.

That great, tolling tone also brought me upright in my bed all through the night, every hour on the hour and at every quarter hour too.

There was a further clanging note: the bathtub was in the kitchen. A very big bathtub in a very, very small kitchen.

I told myself, good sport that I am, that to bathe among the cooking pots was a gay, gypsy thing to do, and so it was. But when the evening chill of the sharpening weather drove me to tubbing at 6 P.M., the atmosphere rapidly thickened to dark-brown Bohemian. Six o'clock, you see, was also the hour when Benjamin's nurse prepared his supper. That kitchen was crowded and cozy, I can tell you, with the nurse frying the chops, Ben playing on the floor, and me bathing in the bathtub, all at the same time.

It was during this period that a most extraordinary phenomenon began to occur—the landlady seemed to materialize in the middle of the sitting room, or even my bedroom, and wordlessly float out the entry door. At first I thought that I'd imagined this specter, but no, Pierre once saw her too. We never spoke, we just followed her with our eyes as she passed silently through the rooms and out.

When we finally learned that our eerie visitor was terrified of small American boys and was sure that Ben would reduce the apartment to a shambles, we realized that what she was doing was patrolling. Then we discovered the outline of a small door which we'd not noticed before, as it was secreted in the damask of Benjamin's room. No knob, no lock, of course, but clearly, at last, this was the passage through which she entered at any odd hour to make her ghostly rounds.

Eventually all that ectoplasmic anxiety and the amount of bath water that was getting into Benjamin's chops and the amount of chop fat that was getting into my bath water brought about the mutually relieving decision that we ought to live elsewhere.

This time I found quite another sort of apartment, on the Right Bank, near the Étoile. It had a long, rather spacious entrance hall, the use of which was strictly limited to the purpose for which it was designed. It also had a sitting room paneled in light almond green, two bedrooms, a kitchen without a bathtub, and bathtub where you'd expect it.

When my new landlady departed on a three-month voyage she confirmed that I could have her apartment only during her absence. I accepted the condition cheerfully. After all, in three months I'd certainly be able to find another, more permanent, abode, and in the meantime, Ben and I would not only be bedding in the bedrooms and cooking in the kitchen, but also, for a change, we'd be sitting in a sitting room and bathing where we ought to.

All went well until the doorbell rang one day and

who should be standing on the threshold but my current landlady. She looked shattered. I looked shattered too. I wasn't nearly accustomed to these phantasmagoric appearances of my proprietresses, I can tell you. In this case, however, we did speak, and I learned that she'd just rushed back over the Atlantic (not by magic carpet, as I recall, but by plane) at the behest of her Paris lawyer. There'd been, she told me, a sudden tightening of restrictions on the subletting of Paris apartments, and she was limited to lending hers to friends. Therefore, she went on to say, to avoid being evicted from these rooms which had for so long been her home, she would have to be in a position, immediately, to prove that she was in occupancy and that a certain American woman and her little boy were merely guests. That night she moved into the sitting room.

Every night thereafter she came in around eleven and went to bed on the couch in that verdant, paneled room. Every morning afterward she and I would meet, in our dressing gowns, for a cup of coffee in the kitchen. It was all rather jolly, really, and pale-green Bohemian this time, instead of dark-brown.

As the third month came to a close, I was lucky enough to find still other quarters, again on the Right Bank, but nearer to the Bois. As in the previous place, we again had an entry just for entering, we had a kitchen without a bathtub, and a bathtub in the bathroom. We also had two bedrooms, a boudoir and, connected by an archway, two rooms which served as sitting room and dining room—but separately. They were ornamented with low-hanging, crystal-dripping chandeliers, tapestries, and dark mahogany Restoration furniture. "Restoration" means, I later learned, the period just after

Napoleon the First, when the French made a try at a monarchy again. Somewhat uneasily, I noted that the walls were hung in rich red damask.

The silvery charm of my most recent landlady, however, put my uncertainties to rest, and I settled down to enjoy both the nineteenth-century elegance of my surroundings and, beyond our windows, the chestnut-bordered avenue with its bridle path, down which rode on Sundays the *Garde Républicaine*, magnificently uniformed in white breeches, dark-blue tunics faced in red, and shining helmets festooned with scarlet plumes. Then one day the landlady came to call.

She had come to tell me, she said, with anxious grace, that a very dear friend of hers, the lady in the apartment immediately below ours, had just died, and that she herself not only anticipated following her friend's example in the very near future, but would like to do so in her own bed. I was stunned. However, I rose marvelously to the moment, I think, and calmed her at once with the clear assurance that I'd do everything possible to accommodate her.

Thereupon, though it was in the dead of winter, I began an intense, shivering and seemingly hopeless search for another roof. All the time, of course, I envisaged our being forced by the imminent demise of our proprietress—and by pure *politesse*—to pitch a tent in the snow-bound bridle path, with the certain result of our being crushed under the Sunday hoofs of the *Garde Républicaine* and of our thus beating our landlady to it.

Then one afternoon I came in, mauve of nose and frozen of foot, to find my landlady there before me. She wished me to know, she gently explained, that she had changed her mind and would not, after all, be joining her friend in another world. I must feel free, therefore, to live on in these Old World, evocative rooms, as she would no longer be needing my bed as a point of departure.

I don't know why I never really felt *secure* after that, do you?

"Ça n'existe pas en France"

14

It wouldn't occur to you, I know, but I've an awful lot in common with Napoleon Bonaparte: exactly the same problem with the French. They kept saying to him that everything he wanted to do was impossible, and they keep saying precisely that to me. With him it was the military, with me it's saleswomen. That time, for example, when Napoleon wanted to get those cannon over the Alps and all his French engineers told him, *"C'est impossible"*—take me any time I want to buy anything, my salesladies say the same thing to me. The difference is, though, that that Little Corsican knew what to say right back, and this little American doesn't. Napoleon knew that what those Frenchmen were looking for was a *"bon mot,"* *"une bonne réponse,"* and he gave it to them. He said, "Impossible is a word found only in the dictionary of fools." The French thereupon not only got those cannon over the Alps, they made him Emperor. Of course, around him they stopped saying the word right then and there, but they didn't stop saying it to other people, and since that day no one else has ever been able to come up with an outwitting witticism to check them. I'm working on it, though, and I've got my coronation robes all set in case I make it.

My saleswomen put me through a double frustration. They not only tell me that it's impossible to buy whatever I'm shopping for, they also tell me that *"ça n'existe pas en France."* My method of dealing with this statement is sheer, grim, dogged persistence. I once went to ten shops in the Avenue Victor Hugo hunting for some perfectly ordinary high rubber boots for Benjamin. Each time, of course, my inquiry was met by the same phrase, and each time the brilliant response which would have procured those boots for me failed to spring to my tongue. Nevertheless, reduced to a glowering *"Merci"* though I was, I marched, round-shouldered but determined, from shop to shop until, at last, I reached the eleventh. There I found the boots. The salesgirl was new at the job.

Yes, there's nothing to do but persist. Not so long ago, having decided that a simple, straightforward, black necktie would look very smart with Benjamin's dark-blue-and-black striped blazer and blue shirt, I charged off to Trois Quartiers to find one. There I was, right in front of the boys' counter asking for a black tie, and as usual the saleswoman stared me right in the eye and told me my request was impossible because a black tie *n'existe pas.* I hoped that this time my coronation *réponse* would leap to my lips, but it didn't. However, I had the advantage just the same, because the ties were above the counter instead of below it, where they usually keep up the game by keeping the merchandise concealed.

"If it doesn't exist," said I in my heavy way, "then what is that hanging behind your shoulder?" She turned, looked, and taking down the article in question, said, "You mean, Madame, a *plain* black tie." She had the last word, but I had the tie.

Once, just once, I enjoyed a splendid vindication. It happened quite by accident. I was in the bedding department at Les Galeries Lafayette and had sat down on a mattress to check over the list of purchases which I had in my hand. I was garbed in my combat shopping uniform of funeral-gray cardigan and skirt and looked, I suppose, exactly like a saleswoman sitting down not only on her job but on her wares. At this moment an elegant, gloved, hatted and fur-coated Parisienne came surging up to me and asked if she could find such and such an article in my department. Quick as a fox, I replied, "*Impossible, Madame, ça n'existe pas en France.*" She gasped and heaved, as I usually do, but then made her way, baffled and broken, toward the escalator. No coronation for *her*.

I think we can conclude that Napoleon never had a concierge, because if he'd had one, his response to what I think of as The Concierge's Complaint would have come down to us as recorded history. The concierge, as you know from all those French novels you've been reading lately, is the elderly lady in faded black who lives on the ground floor of every French apartment house, and whose duty it is to dust the stairs, stoke the furnace, keep an eye on anyone who enters the building, and keep a rich odor of cooking circulating through the halls. To you, as the tenant, she has another obligation, the most sacred of all, and that is to deliver to you, every single day as you leave the building, her comment on the weather. The comment is always negative.

If it should be the first day of spring, a fresh fifty-five degrees in the shade, and a morning so glorious and luminous that you are wearing your new spring costume to celebrate it, the concierge will be waiting for you in the foyer to commiserate on the terrible, unbearable heat.

If, on the other hand, all of France has been suffering from the fiercest drought in five hundred years, if a disastrous water shortage threatens, and the churches are crowded with petitioners for rain, the moment you step upon the doorsill to unfurl your umbrella in joyful greeting of the first, timorous, long-awaited droplet, the concierge intercepts you to remark, "What a deluge, Madame, what a deluge."

Naturally, this prelude to the day's events colors everything that follows, and no matter what good fortune may befall you, enveloped as you are in the gray garment of the concierge's gloom, you take a dismal view. You may try to circumvent her by escaping from the building without attracting her attention. Here, alas, the word *impossible* can be used with dreadful, hopeless justification, because even though you may live on the fourth floor, the concierge knows the very second you pass through your private portals, and she is waiting for you, already arranged in an attitude of sad lament, by the time you reach the *rez de chaussée*.

I know, because for three years I tried every possible

ruse to avoid this grievous trial, and for three years I was defeated daily. Our building being without an elevator, the trick was to get down the staircase unobserved. I tried tiptoeing. Childishly ineffective. I crept down in my stocking feet. A fruitless effort. I shod myself in Indian moccasins and tennis shoes. To no avail. Then I tried a new tack: I tried disguise. The concierge saw right through it. Finally I hit upon the marvelous idea of tying the sheets together and letting myself down through the window. Pierre pulled me back over the sill, pointing out that the line of my descent would take me, fatefully, right past *her* window.

Trapped, I studied not only the collected works of Napoleon, but his military maneuvers too. Nowhere, however, was there the slightest clue as to how the Little Corporal would have handled the situation. At last it was that old saw about Alexander the Great that released me from my dilemma, or rather, his old blade. I remembered that when Alexander was confronted with the hideous convolutions of the Gordian knot it never occurred to him to try to unravel it, but with the single stroke that made him master of the world, he cut smack through it with his sword. In this principle lay my liberation.

Craftily, stealthily, I began house hunting. Secretly, furtively, I whispered to Pierre one afternoon that I'd found just the dwelling we were looking for. Closeted in the hushed dimness of a *notaire*'s office, I signed the documents which gave us possession of a house all for ourselves and all to ourselves. A house, of course, without a concierge.

Silently we went about packing our possessions in the apartment, and finally, on a glowing, golden day in

June, we gathered up the children and our belongings and descended the stairs to run the gauntlet for the very last time.

The concierge, of course, awaited us. And with an absolutely dazzling smile, she said, "Isn't it a lovely day, Madame—a lovely, lovely day!"

Separate candles

15

On a trip home to the United States not so long ago I went through a very extraordinary experience on television. Influenced, I suppose, by the backwash of the McCarthy investigations, the style of the television interview had become, I found to my discomfiture, the style of the third degree. And all sorts of rather banal facts about one's life, when subjected to the accusatory question, seemed to take on, under the interviewer's cold, condemning glare, the most sinister and criminal implications. But I want you to know that once, under the thumbscrew's unspeakable duress, I snapped back with a *réponse* that merits your highest approbation. In fact, since I may never prove myself in France, and run a great risk of never being coronated, I feel that the least that you, my fellow Americans, can do, is make me President. I really have earned it.

Here's what happened. On a nation-wide program,

a green and baleful eye bore down on me and a voice freighted with censure charged me with the following terrible indictment: "Miss de Havilland, we understand that you have two offspring, a boy and a girl, and that you are bringing up the first a Protestant, and the second a Catholic. Do you not think, Miss de Havilland, that this *confused* background is *unfair to your children?*"

Before 20,000,000 people I was appalled. I'd never thought of my conduct as *confused* before, in this regard, and I couldn't imagine the children being upset in any way by having different but intimately related faiths. Furthermore, it had never occurred to me that I could possibly be considered a *bad mother* for what had come about so naturally. As I struggled to reply, I was more than rattled, I was affrighted, for I was certain that if I didn't come up with the right answer I would either be boiled in oil or grilled alive under the supervision of the Inquisitor General and in full view of the television audience. Suddenly, some mysterious force invaded my paralyzed psyche, set my tongue a-going, and I heard myself replying with a certain spirit, "This country was founded on the principle of religious tolerance, and *we* practice it *right in the heart of the family.*" The Inquisitor folded, and just as I was about to throw *her* into a pot of boiling oil, the program came to a close.

All right, now when do you inaugurate me?

However, the question which had hung for such a long, foreboding moment upon the air has, since then, stimulated me to considerable thought about the fact that it was so easy for me, a Protestant, to take Gisèle down to the Church of Saint Honoré d'Eylau in the Avenue Victor Hugo and turn her over to the spiritual ministrations of Monseigneur Sedillière. It is true, of course, that although every Frenchman is born protestant and protesting, almost none would ever dream of being baptized anything but Catholic, and it is also true that it is to this massive majority that my husband belongs. But it was not, I realized after the television program, just to please my husband that I had so blithely and so joyfully delivered my daughter unto Rome. It was also, I decided finally, because I myself had had a quite unique and special training for that particular and portentous moment.

It all began, I think, back in the Convent of Notre Dame in Belmont, California, where the nuns were unwittingly preparing me for more than one of the exigencies of life in France. Just as surely as she was investing me with the staying powers of a camel by saying, "No!" every time I raised a desperate "May I . . . ?" hand in class, Sister Mary Constancia was insuring in still other ways my happy adaptation to a country which is fully 95 per cent Roman Catholic.

She did it by the sagest of rules. She said that all the little Protestants in the convent (five in the primary grades) *must*, absolutely *must* get up at 5:30 in the morning with all the little Catholics, to go to Mass. The rule was marvelously clever, because if all the little Protestants had been allowed to stay in bed, can you imagine the falling away there would have been among the faithful? There was only one exception to the rule: Protestant or Catholic, you could remain in bed if you had taken castor oil the night before. Naturally, on first learning of this dispensation I took immediate advantage of it and swallowed a tablespoon of castor oil for five nights in a row. In the long run and in the short, however, I found the practice rather fatiguing, and finally gave it up. I developed, at last, the true school spirit.

It seemed to me, moreover, that the Mass was a perfectly awesome and beautiful ceremony—the flowers, the candles, the incense, and the splendid robes of Father Greene were to me the ultimate in what was poetic, mystical, and romantic. We will not go into my conduct, however, the time the cat got loose behind the altar.

When I entered the convent, I did so under a decided handicap. My sister Joan, fifteen months younger than I, had been there for six months just before me, and with the really beastly shrewdness that younger sisters are wont to have, she had had a *vision*. Right there, during Mass, she had seen the Virgin Mary, and had immediately fainted. Of course, the nuns were in a dither of excitement about it, and Joan, who had already earned among them the gentle appellation "duckie," departed from the convent at Christmastime with their tender blessings, leaving behind her an aura of unsurmountable prestige. Now, you just try following to a convent a younger sister who has had a Vision. Just try it.

Once established in the convent's strict and reverent routine, I waited and waited to have a manifestation of my own. Nothing happened at all, except that Sister Mary Constancia had a vision of what she considered a really degrading nature during Physical Ed., and as a result I was detained after class to write one hundred times on the blackboard, "Henceforth I will always be a lady and will never again show my bloomers while playing basketball." She called me, as I remember it, a "brass monkey." Not even *her* brass monkey. *A* brass monkey.

Anyway, when it became clear to me that the Virgin Mary was feeling rather reticent and would not immediately help me to attain the same prestige which she had so indulgently bestowed upon my sister, it occurred to me one day that what she wanted me to do was render her a service before making her appearance.

At that very moment I happened to be in her Grotto in the convent grounds, and as the thought struck me, I noticed simultaneously that the Grotto was crawling and encrusted with disgusting little garden snails. "What an offense they must be to her," I exclaimed. They were, immediately, an offense to me too. In our garden at home I had seen similar snails, and the family custom was to pour salt upon them, to which they would react by boiling up into a froth and subsequently evaporating. Instantly, I understood what I must do to bring about the Visitation of the Virgin. I must dedicate myself to ridding the Virgin's Grotto utterly and completely of those blemishing, abhorrent and sacrilegious snails.

I became wily and resourceful in the pursuit of this holy enterprise, and promptly organized a chosen band of mixed Catholics and Protestants to assist me every noon hour, immediately after lunch and just before our first afternoon class, to wage this battle of the innocents.

The problem, of course, was to obtain the salt. I solved it. I instructed my small army to remove from the luncheon table, every day and without being observed, every one of the saltcellars thereon. I told them not to put the cellars in their pockets where the nuns would easily detect them, but to secrete them in their bloomers. My crew was then to meet me in the Grotto and join me in the attack, and at the first sound of the class bell, restore the cellars to their bloomers. At the evening meal, they were surreptitiously to return each shaker to the table.

The plan worked brilliantly for a full week. Snails

were foaming up all over the Grotto and turning into vapor, and in my imagination I saw this sacred place clean of its blemishes, and I myself favored at last, in full Mass, before the entire school and all the nuns, and even Father Greene, with a glorious Appearance of the Holy Mother.

In the meantime, of course, consternation reigned among the nuns. After every noontime meal, no saltcellars remained upon the table. After every dinnertime repast, the saltcellars were back in their accustomed places. Alas, the finger pointed inexorably to the Brass Monkey. The Brass Monkey was questioned, the plot exposed, and all the saltcellars were ordered restored without further delay to the refectory table, never to be removed again no matter how noble the cause, under pain of having to write two hundred times upon the blackboard another humiliating legend.

Of course, I never did have the Vision. My great work had not been completed, you see, and I do think the Virgin Mary does like things to be perfectly tidy before she gives such a special benediction.

My contact with the Mother Church was less intimate after I left the convent, but the ground, if it had not been sanctified, had at least been salted.

One day after I had taken up residence in France, and I discovered from Benjamin's otherwise praiseworthy report card that his *soin* and *écriture* were *mal* (his neatness and writing were *bad*), I took him by the hand in the lovely Normandy village near which he goes to boarding school and where I lunch with him on Sundays, and I said, "Ben, because I don't see a Protestant one anywhere around, you are going with me into that ravishing twelfth-century Roman Catholic church in the square, and you are going to pray for a little heavenly assistance with your *soin* and *écriture*."

Benjamin was horrified. He protested that he wouldn't even *go* into a Catholic church. "Why," he gasped, "they don't even have so much as the same *Bible* that we do."

"Never mind," said I with firmness. "In such a time as this, it is not the differences between the faiths which interest me, it's the similarities."

We entered the church, which, at two in the afternoon, was quite deserted, and as I strode round looking for the proper place to address a few words of intercession, I noticed that one saint had an extraordinary number of *plaques de remerciement* (tablets saying "thank you") embedded in the wall behind her—thirty-nine in all, whereas the others had, at most, only nine. I had no idea who this remarkable personage might be, but I said to Ben, "Clearly this is the saint to address your plea to. She's a whizz—you can see that for yourself. Here's a saint who gets things done." Very dutifully, Ben knelt down, folded his hands, closed his eyes, and you could see that he was doing a lot of very earnest silent praying.

Two weeks later, when we were again together in the village, Benjamin pulled from his pocket his most recent report card and handed it to me. I examined it with tense eagerness, my eyes rapidly running down the subjects until they reached *soin* and *écriture*. Alongside those two words was the miraculous observation *"Bien."*

"Well, Ben," I said, exhilarated, "you have certainly found yourself a friend." And I immediately inquired at the local bistro who the saint was with the thirty-nine *plaques de remerciement*.

"You mean," came the query, "the one with the red and white roses in her hands?"

"Yes, I think so," I replied.

"Oh," was the answer, "that's Sainte Thérèse de Lisieux."

From that moment on, Sainte Thérèse and I, as is well known among my friends, became much more than mere acquaintances. We have what you might call a working relationship.

Two years ago when I was in California, for example, a Protestant friend of mine who had been having difficulties in his marriage invited me to dine with him. He said, "You know, my wife is in Europe and she simply won't come back. I'm very much afraid that our marriage is at an end and I deeply regret the fact, as I'd very much like it to go on."

I leaned across the table and fixed him with a glowing eye. "You have nothing whatsoever to worry about," I said. "I am leaving for France in a very few days. The minute I get there I will go straight out to Benjamin's school to see him. I will immediately thereafter pay a visit to Sainte Thérèse in the church in the village square. I will, I assure you, light a candle for you and your wife, and your marriage will be restored—you can be certain of it."

I did exactly as I had promised, but four weeks later received a rather querulous letter from the husband to the effect that my efforts had been of no avail. I wrote him immediately not to lose faith. The desired reunion would take a little while to bring about, perhaps, but he could be assured that, in the end, the happy result would obtain. Sainte Thérèse, I explained, was, after all, a European, and therefore could not be expected to have the same sense of time as we Americans. I must say I did have an anxious moment, though, when a letter arrived from the wife saying that in a few days she would be taking the final, decisive step and would be filing suit for divorce. However, on the very eve of the scheduled day, a cable from the husband came winging over the Atlantic, bearing the message, "Sainte Thérèse rides again." The marriage had been restored.

Nevertheless, about six months later, when I found myself again in California, I once more received an invitation from the besieged and beleaguered husband. At the end of the meal, with a grave and disheartened face he confided that he had already given the sad news to Louella and wanted me to know before I picked up the morning *Examiner* that this time the marriage was really at an end and a divorce between him and his wife would soon take place. Furthermore, he was now perfectly resigned to the inevitable, he said, and had already adjusted himself fully, and even with a certain relief, to the idea of a completely new and celibate life. As we parted company, I said to him with utmost sympathy, that I was, as he knew, returning on the morrow to France. That immediately on arriving there I would of course go straight to Normandy to visit Ben, and that I would at once pay a visit to Sainte Thérèse in the church of the village square where, he could be assured, I would light a candle for him and his wife. He paled, clutched my arm and whispered with a hoarse and desperate urgency, "Separate candles! Separate candles!"

I don't know why it is that it should have fallen to me to train Gisèle in the customs of her faith, but the other day when we went to see Ben in Normandy and then around to my favorite village haunt, just outside that lovely edifice, I rehearsed my daughter in the proper conduct of a little Roman Catholic on entering her church. I told her that on coming through the door and seeing the altar she must make a little genuflection, like a curtsy, and that, at the same time, she should make the sign of the Cross with her right hand, touching first her forehead, then her breast, then her left shoulder, and finally her right. She loved the whole idea and practiced energetically. However, when we got into the church, she did as she'd been told, but with much greater fullness than I'd counted on. She bent *both* knees, in what can only be described as a deeply reverent but unmistakable *squat*, and then proceeded to make the sign of the Cross with *both* hands at the same time, starting at different points of the compass and ending up in what appeared to be a sort of sacramental cat's cradle.

I am sure, though, that her radiant spirit can only have charmed the angelic personages who may have been observing her, and I am certain, too, that Sainte Thérèse, herself, was very pleased a little later, when Gisèle rose after having addressed to her her very first prayers, and exclaimed in a ringing and jubilant tone, "*Ça y est!*" or, freely translated, "All set!"

Madame est servie

16

Just as I once did, you have probably been cherishing for years the tender illusion that 75 per cent of the population of the land of the fleur de lys is made up of pert but immaculate French maids just longing to run your home for you in a manner of brisk perfection, with a gleaming smile and an adorable accent, garbed in a smart black uniform set off by spotless white cuffs, collar and apron. That French maid, dear friends, whom you first encountered in a Philip Barry play or a Noël Coward musical comedy, existed at that moment of discovery only in the mind of the playwright. As, dear friends, the present theatrical trend being what it is, she now exists only in yours.

You think you've got your problems in the land of the free but flustered housewife, with nary a hand to help, either with that dinner you've invited those people to on Tuesday evening, or with those wild Indians who have the effrontery to pass themselves off as Boy Scouts but require a reliable adult or adolescent presence on Friday night, when you will be dining down the road with the friend who cannot imagine what she was thinking of when she recklessly asked you. Well, over here, under the broad, bright bands of the tricolor, you can have troubles too. You may be able to get the hand, but the amount of help it will give you, and the style in which it will give it—wait until you *hear*.

Right now, let's take up the bright, capable, well-groomed image you have so vividly fixed in your mind and heart. Yes, let's just do that. As you look yearningly out across the Atlantic, you see her on that far, Gallic shore as clear and fresh as crème de menthe despite the distance: the French Maid, a symbol of beaming efficiency whose sole purpose in life is to be of service to *Madame*. She smiles back at you across the waters, a-quiver to serve you a *Cordon Bleu* dinner which she has not only cooked herself but for which she has even invented the recipes, to keep whatever setting of whatever play in which you see yourself in exquisite order, to maintain not only your own wardrobe but that of *Monsieur* in impeccable condition, and even to *draw your bath*. There she is, a hybrid lady's maid, housemaid, and chef *extraordinaire*. Okay, she's a maid of all work. But elegant. An *artiste*.

Fade out, fade in. You're in France. You're having the devil's own time finding a maid of all work—or what is it they call her over here? Oh yes, "*Bonne à tout faire*"— "good at doing everything." Of course—fits in exactly with your conception of the French Maid: a perfectionist in crisp black-and-white. You are leery of agencies in a foreign land because you've been told that if you engage one of their clients you have to pay the *agency* a month's salary, so you decide to use other means in locating your French Maid. Finally, highly recommended by her friend, the saleslady in that refined little shop which sells embroidery yarn in the Avenue Victor Hugo, you find your gem, your jewel, your pearl. Her name is Françoise. How fitting. Your French Maid at last, and her name so like that of the country of which she is so flawless and so famed a representative.

Françoise arrives *chez vous*, ready to take over, ready to transform your life and household with her precious arts. But you are a little puzzled by the fact that in the dead of winter she is not wearing stockings. Also, although she *is* wearing black, the garment is one which seems to have been in the family for several generations. Furthermore—can it really be? yes, it can—a chestnut-purée-colored turtle-necked sweater emerges from *beneath* the garment's top button. And Françoise has clearly forgotten her white collar and cuffs.

You begin to face a fact or two, and decide that although no French Maid in any American play you have ever seen ever wore anything of the sort, Françoise really ought to have a work uniform for her ordinary duties about the house, so you buy her three very attractive blue-and-white pin-striped garments with three-quarter-length sleeves and a high neck and, you are pleased to note, fresh white collar and cuffs firmly sewn in place. And you buy her three or more well-designed white aprons to go over them.

Françoise receives these articles unemotionally and retires to her room. A little later she reappears wearing the blue-and-white striped dress you thought such an admirable choice, and though the round white collar of the neat little neck smartly encircles her throat, descending from beneath those trim three-quarter-length sleeves are the arms of her chestnut-purée sweater.

Of course, Françoise has forgotten to make use of the apron. She is still without stockings. But she has chosen to wear with her new attire a pair of fleece-lined bedroom slippers—the kind that hug the ankles.

Françoise, you soon learn, talks to herself. She will even talk to herself while you are in the room. She also daily empties a full tin of what must surely be called Old French Cleanser into the bathtub (which, because of your strict upbringing is always a-gleam because you always scrub it after yourself) and then she fails to rinse the cleanser out. She leaves it there so you'll know she's given the bathroom her attention, but in the meantime you are wondering what all that wet cement is doing at the bottom of your tub. Françoise also leaves the duster on the balustrade of the staircase, on a chair, or in the middle of the floor. Françoise also tells you when you are hunting for your small boy's absent pajamas—the three pairs you bought him four weeks ago and which you need to pack because he is leaving for a month in the country—she tells you that they are missing, that they are not in the house, that something must have happened to them. Françoise has put them in her bureau drawer because she has forgotten to iron them, but you will not discover this until you have:

1) bought three new pairs of pajamas,
2) sacked Françoise.

Françoise, although she has not invented the recipe, will attempt a perfectly plain pound cake from *Elle* Magazine, and will bring it to the table in the form of yellow French plastic. Françoise also breaks things. Anything. Everything! You now mention timidly the term, "*Bonne à tout faire*" to a French friend. He lets out a whoop of Gallic mirth and says, "*Bonne à tout casser*, you mean!" With painful comprehension you translate: "Good at breaking everything." In due time, in a welter of broken porcelain, glass, vacuum cleaner parts and empty tins of Old French, you give Françoise "*congé*." In other words, the sack. Well, at least you have three more pairs of pajamas in the house than you'd thought. That's something.

After parting from Françoise you sit down in the winter sun at a small table at a sidewalk café and give the works of Philip Barry and Noël Coward a little careful, ruminative thought. Perhaps, in drawing that keen, able, spruce little personage which has meant so much to you so long, the authors have brought a little dramatic license into play. That is to say, for theatrical economy, to keep the stage clear of a full army of domestic help, have they not, perhaps, *compounded* the gifts, functions, and capacities of the French Maid? As they have let you come to know her? In order, then, to arrive at the true, original model, it follows, does it not, that one must eliminate, or rather, subtract one or more of these gifts, functions and capacities? That *Cordon Bleu* diploma, to be realistic, ought to go. Why not, in fact, drop the whole activity of cooking? Very well, then, the real, true French Maid does not and cannot cook at all. Logical, really—cooks cook, maids maid.

Now, what about the drawing of the bath, the keeping impeccable of the wardrobe of *Madame* and even of *Monsieur*? Come to think of it, if she's so darn competent it might be best to keep her out of and away from the wardrobe of *Monsieur*. All right, let's limit her to the wardrobe of *Madame* and let's keep her concentrated only on the bath of *Madame*, too, while we're about it. These duties would make her—a lady's maid? But what about that trim black uniform with the white collar, cuffs and apron? She can't be a lady's maid in a costume like that, and how well you know, for you will never forget your first encounter with a French lady's maid at that opulent chateau where you were invited to spend a country weekend last month. Your mind paralyzes even now at the recollection of standing there in your bedroom and in your girdle before changing for dinner, and seeing that dour figure framed in the doorway asking you if she could be of any assistance. You couldn't imagine who she was, attired in that aquamarine sports dress as she was. On general principles, you said, "No." Naturally.

It was a lovely idea while it lasted, but you clearly can no longer count on the French Maid to draw your bath and keep your clothes, etc. She simply is not a lady's maid. That leaves you and her with only one remaining possibility: she's a housemaid, who changes into that black uniform, that white collar, those white cuffs and that white apron, to serve at table. That's it. You're on the right track at last.

However, you feel you want a little verification before you make the final identification, the definitive categorization. You will, therefore, be particularly observant the next time you dine in a French home and are served at table by a maid.

Consequently, when Countess X asks you to dinner you accept with unusual alacrity. The evening of the Big Test arrives and you arrive just a little ahead of time *chez* the Countess. You admire her collection of porcelain—a marvel of treasures from Saxe. You take an apéritif from the hands of the maître d'hôtel—well, *he's* pretty neat in his black and white. Now, why hasn't *he* inspired our native littérateurs? Have you ever heard of a French butler in a play by an American playwright? No. He has to be an *English* butler to get into a play by an American playwright.

Dinner is announced, again by the maître d'hôtel. As you enter the dining room and seat yourself you are beginning to wonder if there will, after all, be a maid waiting at table. Then following the maître d'hôtel with the soup plates, she makes her appearance at last.

You give her a fast but comprehensive glance. Wearing black, all right. A black garment. No, it's an *ensemble*. A *sweater* and *skirt*!

Wearing a white collar around the sweater neckline, though. And white cuffs over the ends of the sleeves. Wearing a white apron, too. Maybe this is *she*?

Don't conclude too fast. Check her *feet*. Shod in black, all right. Black. Yes. Tennis shoes.

Minus your
Maidenform bra

17

In no way is the difference between the two cultures, French and American, more evident and more clear than in the attitude of each toward the Bosom. Our American philosophy in this regard can be summed up, it appears to me, as that of the Bosom Rampant. The French, on the other hand, subscribe to the principle of the Bust Trussed.

The two divergent, indeed, opposed ideologies are most vividly and dramatically expressed in the World of Couture and the World of Girls and/or the World of the Girl Show.

I. The World of Couture

As we may have remarked elsewhere, in America we have our clothes and our cars all confused. Lordy, Lordy, why do they both have to have forward thrust and that deep, rich, sponge-rubber upholstery? Now in France . . . let me tell you.

To begin with, ever since coming to live here I've been faithful to the House of Dior, which means that I've known the establishment under the reign of King Christian the First, under Yves Saint Laurent, who became Prince Regent on the royal demise, and under Marc Bohan, the incumbent. And it is a question as to which of the three has tried the hardest and done the most to flatten my bosom. Not permanently, you understand—just while I'm wearing a dress.

The whole thing started at my first fitting on my first Dior dress, designed by His Highness himself. There I was, standing in the fitting room, half-undressed, in merely my stockings, my slip and my bust, and the next minute I was fully clothed and bustless. At first I couldn't think where I'd gone to. Then I was struck rigid by the idea that some sort of instantaneous and lasting transformation had occurred and that I'd suddenly lost forever what is every girl's pride. Springing out of my paralysis and into action, I looked frantically down my décolleté to see what had happened to *me*. Fortunately, I was still there, both of me. But bound. And gagged. Like the Japanese female foot. Or feet, rather. By a framework of net and bone. The dress's basic foundation.

You mustn't think, here, that I have one of those overexuberant superstructures that really needs lashing to the decks to keep it from going overboard. No, no, not at all. It is, rather, the sort that you might call *appropriate*, quite becoming, so it's been said. Neat but not gaudy. However, it's a wonder what the tender encouragement of a well-placed dart can do to put it "*en valeur.*" Therefore, all in favor of tender encouragement, I did not take the matter of my binding meekly, but immediately crossed pins with my fitter in the first skirmish of the Great War of Compression. But each time I advanced my cause by withdrawing a peg from my armature, the fitter would swoop in with a fresh squad of cleats and batten down the hatches tighter than ever. I tell you, there have been times during these forays when it has been my mind that cleaved and my bust that boggled.

Now that we are in the full swing of the third régime of the House of Dior, you would think, wouldn't you, that, pin-scarred and needle-tried, I'd be able to say to you that I'd succeeded in imposing the American silhouette upon at least one dress of French *haute couture*? But I have not succeeded. As I charge into combat, arrayed as I am in the constraining armor of my basic bodice, oxygen starvation defeats me every time. In the end, I always lose my War of Liberation, and the French always win their War of Containment.

But I must say, I do look darn well dressed. And I'm beginning to accept the French notion that a girl's bust really is more important when she's got her clothes off than when she's got them on.

Now, about when she's got them off . . .

II. The World of Girls and/or Girl Shows

Of course, I know just as well as you do that back home in the States if a girl's got a delicate, elfin 32 she has no choice but to commit suicide. If she has a tender, swelling 34, she can, however, enter a nunnery. If hers is a warm and promising 36, she may resign herself to spinsterhood. But with a generous 38, there's hope—she can take exercises. On the other hand, with a cumbersome

40, Hollywood is bound to find her. And with anything over 42, national adulation is assured. We not only have our clothes and cars confused, we have our girls and Guernseys, too. They need the same gallon content to win the Blue Ribbon.

Over here in France, though, they're not all that keen on animal husbandry. At any rate, they do feel that girls are girls and cows are cows. They do not expect them to look identical. They would consider it udderly ridiculous if they did.

You might say that on this side of the Atlantic the emphasis is on, the interest is in, the individuality and design of the ornament, plurally speaking, rather than the size. In the *personality*, you could go so far as to say. The *expression*, even. You know—piquant, delightful, adorable, appealing, pretty, impertinent, charming, nymphlike, graceful, elegant, winning ... I suppose you could go on counting to at least twenty-five without once mentioning that solid, old American adjective *big*.

Just go to the Lido if you don't believe what I'm saying. Yes, it's true, a whole band of beauties does come right out on that stage in that night club and parade around in front of everybody with nothing on from the hips up but their polka dots. No, I did not find it shocking. I expected to, but I didn't. The first time I went there and those belles appeared practically in the buff, I did not slide right under the table from embarrassment as I thought I would. I just sat there calmly and stared. Like everybody else. The whole performance had a surprising sort of charm. And talk about *variety*. A veritable garden of girls. And not a watermelon in the patch.

In other words, at the Lido, if you've got a delicate, elfin 32, you've got a job. A tender, swelling 34, and you've got a contract. With a warm and promising

36, you're still in bounds. But with a generous 38, take shrinking lessons.

All I can say is that, as the last brace went bobbing out of the room, I turned to Pierre with awed astonishment and said, "My word, there was only one set in the lot that you could possibly call big."

"Yes," replied he. "And didn't it look terrible?"

A small hôtel particulier

18

When Pierre and I finally acquired a dwelling entirely of our own in Paris, the abode we chose was a small *"hôtel particulier."* Now, a *hôtel particulier* is what the French call, in a town, a house. I want to make this clear, because there's no sense your thinking that I've gone into the hotel business when I haven't.

The house is situated in an attractive, tranquil street, but in such a manner that the sun rises over the Portuguese Embassy, hits high noon over the Pakistan Embassy, and sets, rather ominously, over the Soviet Embassy. Furthermore, it is just under twenty feet wide. And it rears up for four floors exactly like a chimney. But just the same we think it has a lot of charm.

When I say *four* floors, by the way, I mean what *we* would call four floors but what the French would say were only three. Not out of sheer capriciousness, you understand, but because they don't call the ground floor the first floor, they call it the *rez-de-chaussée*. It says here, in my French dictionary, that *rez* means "level with," and that *chaussée* means "embankment, dike, causeway, submarine shoal, reef, raised part of street or highway." Our *rez-de-chaussée* is not level with any dike, submarine shoal, or reef; it is level with the sidewalk.

By French standards it's a rather young house, having been built just after the reign of Napoleon III; by ours, it's getting on a bit, the date of its construction coinciding as it does with Custer's Last Stand. Consequently, we understood that before moving into it a little overhauling would be necessary—a little reorganizing, too, so as to make life therein with two small children and a father who had been a bachelor for forty-four years a pleasant, and, I might even go so far as to say, a *possible* thing.

To this cause I looked forward with keen anticipation. It would permit me to exercise American know-how. I would contribute to the ancient, aesthetic French culture the unique gift of American organization, the invaluable Yankee sense of the practical. To sum up, I would reveal to the various French *corps de métier* the great American secret of "How We Do Things Back Home."

Now, of course, I already knew that the French individualistic, or rather, anarchistic, spirit tended to create a certain confusion, or even chaos, in any enterprise, but I felt that a calm, orderly, experienced person of American background would be more than able to cope, and that under my direction electricians, plumbers and painters would immediately recognize the superiority of the American Way and fall quickly into line.

In going over the house's needs, Pierre and I decided to tackle the kitchen first. It was a small, thoroughly

French kitchen and clearly needed to be redone. Redone, of course, *à l'Américaine*. I held a conference with an architect who'd agreed to make a drawing of the proposed installation according to my specifications, with the mason who was to put in the tile work, and with the plumber who was to install the sink and water faucets. The sink was especially important, because there simply could not be a dishwasher. I'd learned, fortunately well in advance of this critical moment, that the average French domestic will, when confronted with such an apparatus, give the mistress of the house a long, level look and turn decisively toward the sink. She has *her* pure Louis XIV tradition, too. What was good enough in Louis' kitchen is good enough in hers.

Having convoked my little team, I explained to them that I did not at all admire the French kitchen sink installations as I had seen them pictured in various brochures and in display rooms. I told them that the French kitchen arrangements did not permit the application of the principles of correct dishwashing technique as laid down by Miss Elise E. Kleemeyer, my revered instructor in Domestic Science at Los Gatos High School, Los Gatos, California. I observed that Miss Kleemeyer had always said that good dishwashing practice required, first, a broad surface on the left-hand side of the sink for the stacking of the dishes after scraping. That the first section of a double-partition sink must be reserved for the soaping and the washing of dishes. That the second section must be employed for the rinsing of the dishes in clear water. And that a large surface on the right-hand side of the sink must be devoted to the draining and the drying of the dishes. There was never, I remarked, in the French kitchen displays, sufficient room on either side of the sink to permit the practice of the Kleemeyer procedure.

Although it seemed to me that after my discourse the manner of the architect, the mason, and the plumber was indulgent rather than enthusiastic, the drawing came off the architect's board showing a kitchen with dishwashing facilities just like those that I'd described, and a copy was delivered not only to me but to the mason and the plumber, too. I was immensely pleased.

Not long afterward I went by the house to see how things were coming along. To my great satisfaction I found the mason hard at work constructing the cement support, later to be covered with tile, for the crucially important sink. Then I noted with horror that although the plan for the installation was tacked efficiently to the wall, the support was so arranged that on the left-hand side of the sink a vast plateau of tile work would extend toward the gas plates of the stove, and that the sink, on its right-hand side, would have, rising from its very lip, like one of the towering cliffs of the Grand Canyon, the kitchen wall.

I was undone. Absolutely undone. I got Pierre over. I got the architect over. I got the plumber over. All as witnesses for the prosecution. I confronted them with the plan. I confronted them with the appalling diversionary tactic of the mason. There was a turgid silence. Then the architect fumed. He sizzled. He exploded. It was his position that the mason was entirely in error. Because from his own point of view the support should have been constructed so as to permit a vast plateau to sweep away from the sink on its *right*-hand side, thus allowing the *left*-hand lip of the sink to kiss the gas plates in the most intimate proximity. At once the plumber began *his* diatribe. In his opinion the mason was grossly at fault. Grossly. The support of the entire unit of sink and plateaus should have been constructed on the exact *opposite* side of the kitchen, under the window, next to the refrigerator. "But the plan," I sputtered, "the plan!" And then all went hazy.

As Pierre revived me in the fresh air of the little garden in the rear, it came home to me what, to a Frenchman, the true function of a plan is. What a fool I'd been. Of course a plan is something to be *changed*. That's the whole basic idea of a plan: change. Furthermore, it is the keenest possible challenge to Gallic ingenuity to ring in as *many* changes on it as it can.

But I won my battle in the end. I went over to the house every single day, and sat there all day long, armed with an electric coffee pot, a slab of cheese and a baguette of bread, until the kitchen was executed—*according to plan*. In a way I was ringing on it the biggest change of all. I *followed* it.

My next major adventure was with the electrician. When he, the plumbers, and the carpenter had come to join the mason in the house I was thoroughly entrenched in one of the empty rooms so as to forestall and avert any changes in plan which *they* might have in mind. Also to diminish the number of variations in the ordinary work schedule of the day which, with their resourcefulness, I knew to be potentially unlimited.

That electrician, for example. His lunch hour puzzled me vastly. At five minutes to noon I would do a sort of military checkup on his whereabouts. There he'd be, established cozily in one of the rooms with the Sterno can flaming away under the hot part of his lunch and with his bread and fruit neatly laid out ready for consumption and his wine bottle already one quarter empty. At one o'clock I'd make another inspection and he'd just be putting his orange peels away in the vacant fireplace and preparing, I always assumed, to resume his work. For the next hour he could never be found. He just disappeared. Finally, one day, in an absolute snarl of frustration because the deadline was fast approaching when we'd said we'd leave the apartment and move ourselves and the children into the house, I went on a relentless search of the entire premises for that electrician. I finally found him in front of the house, in the sunshine, having a grand old chat with a neighboring concierge.

I caught his eye, and with what I thought was a charming and engaging gesture of appeal, I waved toward the house. He broke off his conversation, followed me into the house and up the staircase into the room where he'd been working. This time, now that I'd got him located and nailed to the spot, I thought that I'd remain awhile until he really got back into the swing and rhythm of his duties. He opened his tool box. He took out a screwdriver. It came crashing across the room and fell with a clank about two feet from where I was standing. He took out a pair of pliers. They, too, described an arc and came to rest a little closer to what I did not yet realize was the target. When he had emptied the entire tool box and the full range of his utensils lay in scattered disarray about my feet, the thought crossed my mind that the man might be upset. At that moment his entrepreneur arrived, and do you know that that electrician quit the job right then and there? He pointed a wild and accusatory finger at me, told his entrepreneur that he would no longer work on the premises, and that a re-

placement would have to be found, because I had abused
him dreadfully. Indeed, he said, "One is never treated
comme ça en France!"

Well, I've thought the problem over, and maybe it is
best not to use the direct, clear, frank American method
in every situation which one meets abroad. Maybe, in
the conduct of human affairs in a foreign country one
should employ a style more pleasing, shall we say, to
the native temperament. Next time, with an electrician in circumstances such as those in which I so painfully found myself, I would, I think, do the following: I
would take the telephone off the hook. I would go outside. I would say to the electrician with gentle distress
and genuine concern that a lady with a very pretty voice
had telephoned, asking for him, that I had been hunting
everywhere for him for about five minutes, that I hoped
she was still on the line, and that if she were not, she
would at least call him back, soon. You know, that electrician really would stay on the job after that, and all his
tools would stay there, too.

Now we come to the painters. The painters. Excuse
me a moment while I take an aspirin. Perhaps I'd better
lie down a second, too. Where did I put those smelling
salts? Ah, there they are. Steady, now.

Where was I? Oh yes, the painters.

The front of our house had, when we acquired it,
what the French had been calling since before the
war, the Patina of the Centuries. Things are changing, though, and now we just call it grime. In any case,
various experts looked at the material of the façade and
decided that the only way to handle it was to paint it. A
decorator friend of ours advised us that the façade would
be very smart indeed if it were to be painted stone-
gray with white shutters. We conferred with the head

painter, the paint company, and the painter's crew. We all agreed that it was true, the façade would be really lovely if painted a muted stone-gray, with fresh white shutters. We shook hands on it, and I went off to the United States to make a film, assured that when I returned the front of the house would be transformed into a thing of beauty with its splendid new make-up.

I made the picture in three months, and during the period received innumerable letters from Pierre saying that he missed me, the family missed me (curious, but he made no mention of the *corps de métier* missing me), and that work was progressing on the front of the house. Then, just before I took the plane for Paris, came a jubilant epistle to the effect that the work had been completed on the façade, the scaffolding had been removed, and he could hardly wait for me to see the house with its face cleansed of the Patina of the Centuries and wearing its glorious and gleaming new look.

I arrived at Orly on a cold November day. A clear day. Too clear. We reached the house, I opened my eyes for the grand surprise, and saw the front of the house. A rich lemon-pie yellow with deadly nightshade shutters. I went into deep shock, had to be put to bed, and remained in a coma for forty-eight hours. During this period I came to the subsurface of consciousness only when Pierre thrust a straw between my indigo lips, the other end of which he held in a bowl of clearest bouillon — nothing heavy, or it would have been the end of me.

Just as Pierre was about to call for oxygen, I rallied, raised myself upon my elbow, and spoke. "Pierre," said I, "we cannot, we simply cannot, accept the front of the house. We all agreed that it was to be stone-gray with white shutters. It must, absolutely must, be painted just exactly that."

At last, after much wrangling, the painters admitted that, of course, it *had* been agreed that the front of the house would be stone-gray with white shutters, and the work would be done without charge. I stayed in during those crucial days when the work was being redone as I had not yet regained my strength from the initial shock. Finally, the work was completed, the scaffolding was removed, and leaning somewhat on Pierre because of my weakened condition, I walked slowly out to the sidewalk, turned, and looked up at the house. I saw a fresh, gleaming *white façade*, with *stone-gray shutters*.

You would like to feel that I kept those Stars and Stripes flying, wouldn't you? And that I went after them again and again and said, *"Non, non, non, Messieurs, stone-gray* with *white* shutters, until you get it right!" You'd like to think that, wouldn't you? I didn't do that, I'm ashamed to say. Showing the lemon-pie yellow streak in *me*, I said to Pierre, "At least it's pretty. Let's keep it that way." And so we did.

But not for long. Three months later the whole thing began to peel off like a bad case of sunburn. Great ribbons of paint began to strip off and either flap in the wind or fall to the pavement leaving behind on the face of the house a hideous, scabrous pockmark.

Again we had conferences. A series, I mean. With the head painter, with the paint company, with the painter's crew. Eventually they agreed that they'd have to paint the front of the house all over again. The color? I thought, "This time let's be clever, let's say *white* with *stone-gray* shutters, and then they'll paint it just the opposite and we'll get just what we asked for in the first place."

It is now three years exactly since the first job was done. The scaffoldings are up again on the front of the house and workmen are once more busily engaged on the façade. But what has happened is this: when they removed the white paint, and the yellow paint underneath, a great deal of that undercoating of the Patina of the Centuries came away with it too. We found, underneath, the most lovely, creamy white stone you ever saw. So we've sent the painters away and some stone polishers have taken their place. The shutters will remain as they are. I suppose the painters really have won this round, though, because what we'll have is not a stone-gray façade with white shutters, after all, but a stone-white *stone* façade with stone-gray shutters, exactly what they had in mind for us *last* time.

Not so long ago, however, pleased with my victory over the mason, and one or two others I'm too modest to mention, I went to Alexandre's, to have the paint and plaster washed from my hair. There I saw Fleur Cowles, who had just flown over from London to have the same thing done to hers. She, being a very remarkable woman, had just completed the installation of a magnificent London apartment and a sixteenth-century country house both at the same time and in three months flat. When she asked how I was progressing with my housing problem, I said, recalling with satisfaction my Kleemeyer kitchen and other American innovations, "Fleur, I'm redoing France."

"That's nothing," replied she, "I've just redone England."

A slight matter of

nuance

19

When my French teacher, Mademoiselle Henriette Guyot, had finally implanted upon my brain and upon my tongue at least a rudimentary form of French, she felt that the time had come to instruct me in some of the niceties of the practice of the language, and in the precise meaning of certain phrases in common use. It was during one of these sessions that I learned to my surprise that among the small supply of French expressions— such as *savoir faire*, *comme ci*, *comme ça*, and *au revoir*— which we Americans so habitually employ in ordinary English conversation that we seldom exercise an English substitute, there was one term which means not at all what I thought it meant. The phrase is that familiar pair of words *faux pas*. It appears that what I thought I had so often committed back home—and what, indeed, I have continued to commit over here—was not a *faux pas* at all, but was, instead, a *gaffe*. In response to my startled expression of disbelief, Mademoiselle Guyot carefully explained that a girl had committed a *faux pas* if, for example, she had allowed a man to go just that one step too far before marriage. What I have been limiting myself to over here, as I say, is the committing of *gaffes*. See that you do the same.

Some of my more monumental *gaffes* have been occasioned by the assumption that the holidays at home and their counterparts in France have an identical nuance of meaning and the same manner of celebration.

During my first Parisian fall, as the merry fete approached which is known to readers of the *Herald Tribune* comic page as the Eve of the Great Pumpkin and having already realized that the appellation Halloween, under which it had annually enlivened my California childhood, must mean in uncontracted, older English, All Hallows' Eve, I assumed that the coming holiday, Toussaint, or All Holy, meant exactly the same thing. I was aware that the day itself was of sufficient significance in France to excuse the children from attending school, an indulgence designed, so I presumed, to let them rest after the giddy exertions of the night before. I did not know that it was in order to permit them, garbed not in sheets but in their ceremonial best, to visit in broad daylight rather than by the light of the moon, the family graveyard; and there to lay upon the monuments of the departed, not the eerie relics of mirthful daring, but respectful bouquets of traditional flowers. I did not know that Toussaint is, in France, the very most solemn Holy Day of all.

Thus oblivious to the pitfalls of the season, I accepted without a tremor the pre-Toussaint invitation of Carmen Tessier, whose column, *"Les Potins de la Commère,"* appears daily on the front page of *France*

Soir and whose power and prestige as a lady journalist are unequaled in all of Europe. She had asked us to a *"pendaison de la crémaillère"*—literally, a "hanging of the pothook," a housewarming—at her new apartment in the Street of the Acacias, and, as an innovation in Parisian entertaining, a buffet dinner. Alas, some minor but fateful occurrence delayed Pierre and me, and when we arrived at Carmen's door, not only had the pothook definitely been hung but the house had been warmed to maximum heat. Furthermore, the buffet had already been half consumed and, although you may have heard it said that the French are not unduly punctual, the one occasion for which they are always two minutes before the dot is any event having to do with the partaking of food. Out of respect for the cook.

Now, if there is anything I dislike to do, it is to show a lack of consideration toward a hostess, and my dislike is compounded where there might be implied a lack of reverence toward a cook. My exalted regard of the latter may be attributed, I suppose, to my having been the only girl in Domestic Science II to produce in a single lesson three omelets so unacceptable that Miss Kleemeyer advised me to pour them down the sink. In any case, as the Parisian season drew to a climax, so, too, did my remorseful brooding over my having been late at the hanging of Carmen's pothook. Finally, in a convulsion of wholesome readjustment, I threw off my cloak of guilt and dispatched to my erstwhile hostess, in a magnificent gesture of atonement and with the hope that her cook would appreciate same, a superb bouquet of finest florist flowers. The fact that they had so depleted my purse that I was faced with several days of forced fasting seemed to me all the more appropriate to the situation.

When evening came I explained to Pierre between

hunger pangs that although the body might suffer, my spirit was light, for I had that very morning sent off to Carmen as an expiatory offering no less than three dozen of the very most glorious mauve chrysanthemums ever seen. Pierre promptly turned puce and cried, "*Mon Dieu*—and on Toussaint, too! You don't send them to her while she's *alive*—you send them to her when she's *dead*!"

In France, it seems, the chrysanthemum is the most highly cherished blossom of them all—for cemetery use. Since then, Carmen's been decent to me, but distant.

As the gray mists of November blurred the outlines of the city, they softened, too, the painful recollection of my first Toussaint, and rallying at last, I approached Noël with renewed confidence.

We had been bereft of Pierre's mother some months before, and since, therefore, we wanted this Christmas to be a particularly warm and comforting one for Pierre's father, we made plans for the children, the nurse, and ourselves to take the train for Nice, the family seat. Once there, we established ourselves at the Hotel Ruhl, so as to keep the younger generation out from under Grandpère's feet, and yet corralled and available for visits to the little apartment in the Avenue Desambrois just often enough and long enough to cheer an old man's heart.

The traditional duties of planning the Christmas feast had now fallen to me, and I presently realized that Josephine, the family cook for thirty-five years and twice that span in age, now had six members of the household to deal with at the family table instead of the once customary three. And so I decided that I ought to arrange for caterers to deliver, ready to be served, the festive bird and the festive pie on the festive day. Thereupon, I located a caterer for the turkey, and I instructed the Scotch Tea House to provide the mince pie.

The morning of Christmas Day arrived, and under the tinseled branches of the Christmas tree, among the traditional litter of ribbon, paper and squeals of infant joy, performing the offices of Père Noël which the senior years of his life had so unexpectedly and fortuitously thrust upon him, Grandpère grew rosy with delight.

When one o'clock came round, his appetite whetted by the morning's domestic excitements, he took his place at the head of the table and the rest of us disposed ourselves in an eager and hungry circle around him. When the soup had been served and its dishes cleared away, Josephine brought in with a flourish and set before him as the climax of the day, the triumphant bird. And in due time she capped the climax by placing before him the impeccable pie.

Now, while Pierre and the ominivorous children regaled themselves with these superlative dishes, and the nurse, who was Alsatian, rewarded them with a lively eye and an appreciative fork, my own satisfaction was not complete. Although there never was a more perfectly chosen turkey in this world, nor more perfectly cooked, not better presented, and although there never was a finer mince pie, nor served at more precisely the temperature at which a mince pie tastes best, neither bird nor pie pleased Père Noël. He barely tasted the first, and his single, hesitant forkful of the second elicited from him only the murmured comment, "*Intéressant.*" Wherein had I failed?

Alas, it appears that with infinite care and tenderest foresight I had confronted Père Noël with the very first mince pie of his life and the first Christmas Turkey of his eighty-one years. In old Nice, it turns out (and I do think I may be forgiven for not having guessed), traditional Yuletide menu is—chicken and ravioli. As might be expected, I went into seclusion after that.

I emerged, eventually, for the celebration of the New Year, telling myself that a quiet dinner in one of Nice's better bistros could not possibly hold for me the slightest danger of disaster. I had not counted on my unlimited resourcefulness. As the headwaiter pulled out our table at the banquette on the left, I slid behind it to take the place furthest along the wall. Pierre instantly grabbed my hand, pulled me back and, rounding the table's other end, took the place I'd aimed for. I sat down stunned. What *gaffe* had I committed this time?

"Don't you know," said Pierre, "that a man always seats a lady on his right? In a restaurant, if he places her on his left, it's a signal to all his friends that she's the type he doesn't care to introduce!"

Now I am emphatically for respect and all that. But there are times and places where I think Pierre carries the rule too far. I just can't stand the righthand side of the bed.

Robert E. Lee
in Paris

20

A lot of people have asked me from time to time whether or not I've become an expatriate. My first reaction to that question is a strong impulse to whip out my Smith & Wesson and drill them full of apertures. It always sounds as if they've said ex-patriot. And of course you can't say a thing like that to the mother of a half-Texan. In our family we remember the Alamo.

But I will say that bringing up a full-blooded American, half-Texan boy, who speaks English like Charles Boyer, and inculcating in him his American heritage far from the native land, does pose problems. To do it well requires a certain effort and an organized plan.

First, you decorate his room with photos and miniatures of as many ancestors as you can muster up out of his paternal archives. Over the radiator you range his Great-great-grandmother Norton in her widow's weeds, surrounded by her small daughters, and you explain that all five of them were in Atlanta during The Burning. Over the mantelpiece you hang his great-great-grandfather, Dr. Benjamin Briggs Goodrich, who not only attended the wounded during Texas' fight for independence but who signed in a flourishing hand the very declaration of that independence itself, as well as the Constitution of the Republic of Texas. You mention that you are sorry not to have a photo of his Great-great-uncle John who, of course, actually fell at the Alamo with Davy Crockett and all those other friends of John Wayne. Next to the doctor, naturally, you place his wife, Great-great-grandmother Serena, and under them their son Briggs, who was Attorney General of the Territory of Arizona, and very fast with *his* Smith & Wesson, so they say. Above your son's desk you suspend the very latest model United States flag with every last star in place, and, out of respect for the boys in gray as well as the boys in blue, you hang beneath it the red field and crossed, star-studded bands of the Flag of the Confederacy. You are now ready for the Comprehensive Historical Sketch.

You start with the adventures of Eric the Red, Columbus, and the founders of the Jamestown settlement, passing on through the landing of the Pilgrims, the formation of the thirteen colonies, the Declaration of Independence, the Revolutionary War, George Washington, the Father of Our Country, whose statue is conveniently located in the center of the Place d'Iena, and Benjamin Franklin, whose statue is conveniently located near the Place de Trocadero, and you continue on down through the decades to the present, always emphasizing the principles of liberty for which we stand, the original model of the statue of which is conveniently located in the middle of the Seine.

In the meantime, your son, in his quiet infant way, is busy steeping himself in modern American *culture*. But it takes you a while to realize that his passionate attachment to the character whose name you understand to be Mie Quai Mousse and whose adventures appear in illustrated magazine form at every Paris kiosk on every Thursday, is, indeed, a devotion to none other than our very own Mickey Mouse.

However, learning of your patriotic task, and to make it easier and carry it a step further, friends from the homeland send, every Christmas and every birthday, volumes depicting the lives of great American heroes, great personages in the political and literary development of our country. You read these aloud to your son, cozily, through the summer vacation, the Christmas vacation, and the Easter vacation, and get quite an education yourself.

However, in my case, I've discovered that not every vaunted figure of American fame, no matter how carefully he may have been chosen by the publishers of boys' books, is really the ideal influence for your fledgling patriot 'way over here on a foreign shore. There is only one hero, indeed, whom I have found to be perfectly flawless, and a boys' study of whose life I can recommend without hesitation or reservation. And I'm really an authority, too, for I've read that life out loud exactly eleven times.

The hero of whom I am speaking is Robert E. Lee. He never, absolutely never, did anything wrong. He always told the truth, was a whizz at his studies, was nice to his mother, did the household shopping without complaint, and once, at the age of ten, when he lost five pennies on the way to market, he devised a geometrical technique for recovering them, and found every single cent. He had even freed his slaves long before the War Between the States, and the reason why he chose to defend the South was the logical fact that he lived there.

Now, Andrew Jackson, I am sad to say, does not stand the test. As you read aloud in hushed tones the story of this legendary figure, once President of our fair land, you come abruptly across all that horseracing. You try hurdling that chapter by passing instantly to the next, but your boy is too quick for you and reins you up short. You try to make yourself unintelligible by stepping up your gait to a fast canter, but beagle Ben asks you to pace the course over again. As his eyes gleam, you shudder, for he has the exalted look of a boy who has found his ideal, a boy who is about to *pattern* himself. Long before you reach the end of the book you find your son lying on the floor with the *Herald Tribune*, not engaged, as has been his habit, in a total concentration on the comic page, but in a fascinated study of the page adjoining. He is utterly absorbed by the mad excitements of the high jumps and the low of the United States Stock Exchange.

As you rapidly recite the last page of *The Life of Andrew Jackson*, you close the book firmly and immediately pick up *The Life of Mark Twain*, hoping to erase as quickly as possible the impression which the political figure has made by imposing vividly upon it the image of the literary one.

Alas, you have gone from bad to very much worse. Mark Twain *hated* his studies and *loved* to play truant. Your son's eyes develop that gleam of adulation all over again, and your voice goes hollow as you lead yourself further and further into the mire, trying to recover the situation by commenting with your false, nervous laugh, "Such a *silly* boy, isn't he, when studies are so much *fun*, aren't they?" You plow doggedly on because you know you will make Mark Twain infinitely more interesting if you abruptly stop reading as if you were *afraid* of something.

But the damage has been done. Maximum damage. Your son's next report card comes home with the following notation from the headmaster: "*Benjamin essaye à faire l'école buissonière—*" ("Benjamin tries to play hooky.") We know whose fault *that* is, don't we?

On his next vacation you decide that the very best thing you can do is reread out loud the *Life of Robert E. Lee.* So, once again, you get him to take an hour's rest in the afternoon with the argument that boys grow faster when they're lying down. You then seat yourself in his plaid armchair and begin reading the story of that great gentleman, that boon to mothers far from the native shore, Robert E.

As you proceed you look hopefully to see if Benjamin's eyes are a-shine again. Just as you reach the place where Robert has decided he wants to go to West Point, you think you detect the hint of a glow in his orbs. You plunge into the chapter which follows with full animation, reading with vivid expression, making the whole experience sound thrillingly interesting, desirable, emulation-worthy. When you finish, you look up and find Ben gazing at you with speculation and expectation. And you realize what you've done. You have just given an Academy Award rendition of the account of how Robert's mother, her heart beating with proud encouragement, personally urged her son to go all the way to Washington to call on the Secretary of War; of how she, personally, went to see the one person of influence among their acquaintances whose letter of introduction would insure the Secretary of War's re-

ceiving Robert once he got there; and once he did get
there, how she, personally, canvassed all their friends,
acquaintances and neighbors of note to write the character references which the Secretary had asked for; and
how, indeed, her magnificent *personal* efforts helped to
bring about the realization of her son's dearest wish, his
appointment to West Point. You are aghast. Especially
as Benjamin now confides that he has, indeed, just decided that his new, deep, solemn ambition *is* to go to
West Point.

What can you do? It is clear what you must do. You
have succeeded in getting your son back on the safe
and narrow—for the moment he has forgotten Andrew
Jackson, and the memory of Mark Twain has been oblit-
erated; you must at all costs grasp the nettle firmly and
confirm your son in the image and the footsteps of the
virtuous, the righteous, the admirable Robert E. Lee.
You then say, "Ben, if it's West Point you want, you know
that Mother will do everything possible to see that you
get that appointment. But you know, too, don't you, that
Robert's grades in all his subjects were especially high
ones, particularly so in arithmetic? Therefore, you must
now, when you go back to school, do everything in your
power to see that your own grades measure up to his,
and do all that is necessary to make yourself *eligible* for
West Point." He says with new resolution and decision
that he will. His next report card nearly floors you. He
has "*Très bien*" in *everything*. Including conduct. Robert
was also a very good boy, as we know.

At this moment you realize with fresh awareness the
acuteness of your situation. You are about to leave for
the United States of America for the exploitation of a
film you've made and the title of which at such a time as

this strikes you as painfully apropos—*The Proud Rebel*. It is perfectly clear what your additional and, indeed, primary responsibility will be when you set foot on American soil. You must, without any question at all, emulate the mother of Robert E. Lee. Your eyes may gleam at this realization, but it is not with the fever of adulation, it is with the tear of desperation.

In the States luck is with you. You have a day off from the exploitation schedule to go to Washington. This is even more than Mrs. Lee ever did—she merely urged *Robert* to go there. Enormous good fortune finds you actually in the rear area of the White House. This again tops Mrs. Lee. Then the smiling fates cause your path to cross that of the Secretary to the Cabinet, the charming and affable Robert (there are nothing but Roberts in this story) Gray. You consider his last name, Gray, coupled with his first a good omen. If he'd been Robert Blue things would not have augured well.

Graciously, Mr. Gray asks you if you would like to see where the Cabinet meets. This is almost exactly what you do want, and you almost tread on Mr. Gray's heels as you follow him breathlessly into the Cabinet Room. It is empty. Empty of the Secretary of the Army, the Secretary of the Air Force, the Secretary of the Navy, and of the Secretary of Defense. Empty of all the Secretaries. Of course, it is only the Secretary of Defense in whom you are interested as you assume it is he who has replaced Mrs. Lee's Secretary of War. And the Secretary of the Army might do in a pinch.

You ask Mr. Gray if you might just for a second sit in the *chair* of the Secretary of Defense. He permits you to, and you do feel a little closer to the situation upon doing so. But it is not, after all, quite close enough. You know that if Mrs. Lee had got this far, she would have seen to it that the Secretary was in the chair, and she seated next to it. Mr. Gray is somewhat mystified by your curious absorption in the chair of the Secretary of Defense and, though he is too discreet to say so, would clearly like to know the explanation. You turn a tragic eye on him and explain that you have the solemn responsibility of investigating the steps and procedures necessary to obtain for your brilliant son, whose heart is determined to sacrifice itself in the service of his country, an appointment to West Point. "Oh," says Mr. Gray, "if it's information about West Point that you need, right here in the White House we have a military adviser, Colonel Schultz, who would be just the man to counsel you. Shall I find out if he can see you?" Your "yes" fairly leaps down his ear.

Colonel Schultz *is* able to see you a few minutes later, and down you go to his office, giving the Secretary of Defense's chair a little knock for good luck as you leave the Cabinet Room. Colonel Schultz is an angel. Well, he is already wearing wings on his shoulders, which may have something to do with it. What happens next ... well, perhaps we should let Leonard Lyons and the *Reader's Digest*, who heard about it, tell the rest.

On a trip to Washington, film star Olivia de Havilland confided to the President's aide, Col. Robert L. Schultz (Robert Lee Schultz, perhaps?): "I have a son who wants to go to West Point." The Colonel nodded. "He has an aptitude for engineering," the screen star continued. The Colonel nodded again and asked about the applicant's school grades. "He has an A-plus average," she said. The Colonel, impressed, inquired about the applicant's extracurricular interests, and she told him, "He's working on a missile which will prevent other missiles from reaching their targets."

The Colonel quickly reached for a pencil and paper. "What's his name and age?"

"His name is Benjamin Briggs Goodrich," said Miss de Havilland. "He's eight and a half."

Postscript to the
2016 Edition

An Interview with
Olivia de Havilland

First published in 1962, *Every Frenchman Has One* humorously recounted Olivia de Havilland's first years in Paris in the 1950s. Despite her early skirmishes with the French people, French customs, and the French language, she's lived there ever since. In May 2016, on the occasion of her forthcoming centennial birthday, Miss de Havilland reflected on the book, and what she's learned during her sixty-plus years in the City of Light.

From Vincente Minnelli's An American in Paris *to Stanley Donen's* Charade *and beyond, Paris has been the site of many memorable films over the years. What is it about the city that makes it so irresistible to Hollywood (and to foreigners, in general)?*

To begin with, Paris is a low city with a wide spacious sky above it.

Many of its buildings are ancient, historic, palatial, and beautiful. Furthermore, most of them are faced with luminous, creamy, Parisian limestone. Even my little house, built only a century and a half ago and made of brick, possesses a façade of this lovely material. With wonderful attentiveness, the city requires that these pleasing and ubiquitous exteriors be cleansed every ten years.

There are parks everywhere, creating further open spaces. As does the river Seine, which winds its way through the city, contributing its own special charm wherever it goes.

There are also beautiful squares, like the Place Vendôme, built in 1702 and designed by the great architect Jules Hardouin-Mansart.

A favorite thoroughfare of mine is the Avenue Foch, a broad residential street lined with lawns, flower beds, shrubs, trees, narrow auxiliary throughways, and attractive dwellings. It begins at the Arc de Triomphe, commissioned by Napoleon in honor of the Revolution and the Napoleonic Wars, and, in wonderful contrast, ends in a forest: le Bois de Boulogne.

A love of nature is evident everywhere in this city which has everything to appeal to one's imagination and all one's senses.

Could this explain its appeal to Minnelli, Donen, Hollywood in general, and strangers everywhere?

Did you ever visit Paris as a child? If so, how did the experiences of your youth compare to those of your adult years?

Alas, I never did visit Paris during my childhood. However, when I was five years old my mother did teach me a little French child's song. It had something to do with having in one's right hand a rose.

Years later, when my own daughter, Gisèle, was the same age, I found among the books that friends had given her a collection of French songs for children. Within its pages I came across the very song my mother taught me—the one about having in one's right hand a rose.

Was it easier or more difficult to be a Hollywood celebrity in Paris? How so?

It was marvelous to be a Hollywood celebrity in Paris. Only a small *coterie* of friends had any idea who I was. Wherever I went nobody else recognized me.

I had regained a precious property: anonymity.

Given the perennial interest in books by Parisian women, it seems that les parisiennes *know something about living a good life that American women want to learn. What are the most important lessons—whether about health, love, art, style, food, or anything else—that you've learned from Parisian women?*

The importance of tact, restraint, subtlety, and the avoidance of banality.

In Chapter 7, you refer to the guiding philosophy behind Parisian style as the "Paris principle." In your opinion, what are the key tenets of this principle?

1. Discretion
2. Discretion
3. Discretion

Whom do you consider an icon of the Parisian way, and why?

Madame Anne-Aymone Giscard d'Estaing, the wife of the twentieth President of the Republic of France, Valéry Giscard d'Estaing, 1974 to 1981.

In 1977 Madame Giscard d'Estaing created a foundation under her name, Fondation Anne-Aymone Giscard d'Estaing, dedicated to helping children in need. This later became La Fondation pour l'Enfance, in support of which she initiated annual gala dinners held in l'Orangerie at Versailles, events which people attended with pleasure and enthusiasm.

In the book, you move to Paris, not just as a wife, but as a mother. In your experience, how do French parents differ from American ones? Did you learn anything useful from these differences?

Generally speaking, it seems to me that the French are even more attentive to their children's upbringing than we are.

A custom I found very surprising and delightful was the weekly academic day off: it was Thursday. I inquired as to why it was on this day that grammar school students were excused from class. The reply was this: "It is Grandmother's Day."

Are there any things that Parisians could learn from Americans?

How to fix things.

What advice would you give to a woman who's moving to Paris today?

Take a crash course in French well ahead of time.

Buy a French/English–English/French dictionary before you take the plane.

The book's provocative title comes from one of your witty observations about Frenchmen. What else have you learned about Frenchmen in the past sixty years?

If a Frenchman is tender, his tenderness cannot be equaled.

If a Frenchman is considerate, his consideration cannot be matched.

If you are loved by the French as a whole, you really feel loved.